TRUTH-WROUGHT-WORDS

From

Wahrspruchworte

TRUTH-WROUGHT-WORDS

WITH OTHER VERSES
&
Prose Passages

RUDOLF STEINER

Translated
by
Arvia MacKaye Ege

ANTHROPOSOPHIC PRESS

Copyright © 1979

by Anthroposophic Press, Inc.

All rights reserved. No part of this book may be reproduced
in any form without written permission from the publishers,
except for brief quotations embodied in critical articles
for reviews.

CONTENTS

Note on the Cover Design	vii
Foreword	1
From *Wahrspruchworte*, Truth-Wrought-Words	7
Verses for Children	79
Verses for the Dead	87
The Foundation Stone *(two renderings)*	99
From the Mystery Dramas:	113
Verse passages from	
"The Portal of Initiation"	115
"The Soul's Probation"	134
"The Guardian of the Threshold"	150
Prose Passages	
Concerning and including	
The Dream Song of Olaf Åsteson	163
From the Ancient Norwegian	
Concerning	
Beauty, Truth, Goodness, Love and Freedom	177
Quotation References	201
Index	203

NOTE ON THE COVER DESIGN

The design which appears on the cover was made by Rudolf Steiner for the Seelenkalender, Calendar of the Soul, *in 1924, only a few days before his death, and so was his last graphic form for any book.*

He made two slightly varied sketches for the design, and it is believed that this is the first time that a rendering of this particular sketch has been published.[0] *The other variation was printed in gold on a sky-blue background, and was used again for the first publication of* Wahrspruchworte, *brought out by Marie Steiner soon after his death.*

The design has therefore been chosen once more for this English translation of most of these verses, together with other poems and prose passages collected here under the title: Truth-Wrought-Words.

CONTRIBUTORS
TO THE PUBLICATION OF THIS VOLUME

The translator is indebted to the advice and unsparing help of Christy Barnes in the preparation and perfecting of this volume, as well as to the meticulous proof-work of Sandra Sherman, and wishes to acknowledge most gratefully the contributions made by Dietrich Asten, Anne Barnes, Mildred Gesse, Kathryn Gunzinger and Betty Lipin, which have brought about a fuller text and more beautiful format than would otherwise have been possible.

FOREWORD

The translations in this volume have been made in response to various requests over a period of years, from the 1920's onward. As they are still often asked for, they are gathered together for publication at this time.

Those familiar with Rudolf Steiner's work will be aware that no translation of his mantric verses can hope to render what flows in the original. Yet as they belong to the spiritual literature of humanity, the striving to make what lives and speaks in them accessible in other languages becomes an essential task. And in this struggle, they offer an archetypal training-ground for apprenticeship in the mysteries, use and redemption of language. When language everywhere is undergoing such disintegration as is found today, involvement in such apprenticeship gives rise both to gratitude and to an inward restraint which become intrinsic companions on this path of opportunity. For the fonts from which these verses spring are so inexhaustible and yet of such an exacting and majestic nature, that the goal both brightens and retreats the further we go.

The task, we become aware, is a rare schooling in freedom. For to carry such a source across the gulf from one language to another calls for a very delicate balance of head, heart, and will.

The intellect must become dissolved, yet thought come to life in highest clarity. Feeling must become so fine an organ of light and warmth that it can see into the sounds, can flow with and into the rhythms. And will must weigh and walk, build and mould anew, with courage, selfless surrender, joy, and unending perseverance. Only the activity of creative freedom, using the delicate instrument of "moral intuition," can hope to approach the solutions which beckon here with such powerful and challenging encouragement.

With any work of translation, we must first immerse ourselves in the one language and then dive across an emptiness into the qualities of the other, seeking for the means by which to render again the given passage. In the scientific and intellectual sphere, this requires literal exactitude and minute precision. As soon as we approach the artistic and poetic, however, these qualities are inadequate, for life-forces now come into play, forces which are in constant growth, movement, and transformation. What is said does not have merely one hard and fast meaning; and the sounds and rhythms with which it is expressed play a major role in revealing something which actually is not expressed at all, but is unveiled through their power.

In this case, the activity of passing from one language to the other becomes much like a digestive process out of which new life-forces spring. It is as though we must constantly be ground to bits, dissolve and die into a void, out of which what was at work in the original substance seeks, together with us, for fresh, resurrecting life-forces in which to clothe itself, and at length, through this mutual activity, emerges again into view, rewrought, having woven and "become" its own new translucent garment, while at the same time remaining actually ever hidden. And in this process of constantly diving and leaping again into the light, as a porpoise swims, the whole wonder and quality of both languages as they come into play are like a symphonic ocean upon which to chart our course.

In the case of Rudolf Steiner's verses, however, this challenge meets us in a heightened degree. For, as he has often mentioned, in mantric verses the sounds are at their rightful places; structure and rhythm are born of spiritual reality. The whole is a starry script in which living thought and being are embodied.

"Translation" here is not possible. And yet, just in dedication to the impossible, in inner freedom, the heart can be stirred to offer its efforts on the path of language, sheerly for the love of these verses themselves and in trust that in the struggle the spiritual reality itself, together with the living genius of language, will come to its aid and will do what they alone can do. The outcome then is no longer the significant factor, but the doing, and the becoming. And out of all that can be encountered on this course — the struggle and pain of incapacity, where at first we appear to be quite alone — gradually three main guiding elements emerge.

The first is the realization that the more open we can leave language to harbor many meanings — that is, the less literal it is in the intellectual sense — the more the abundance of the spirit is able to speak through it. While the more we can choose Anglo-Saxon words, and avoid those of Latin derivation, which tend to contribute a more intellectual character, the better we can approach the vitality and power inherent in the original German.

The second is — while living with the music, form, and color of the sounds, the flow and character of the rhythms, their majors and minors, impetus and contraction, power and reticence — the need to develop, as these are taken into the experience of the heart, the capacity for stillness: to listen — to ask — to listen — and to wait — even for very long. In this way it is possible to enter into and give over our efforts to that stream of timeless expectancy where moral intuition and its companions, inspiration and imagination, are active, and able at the appointed time to grant their gifts. For only out of the void of death can these messengers cause the wonder-web of sound, rhythm, and content to arise afresh, woven in the new language, so that it can breathe and live, and not be misshapen and maimed.

The third is the need for the exercise of the strictest truth and devotion toward the spiritual reality embodied in the original verses, its content and being in all its fullness — not an adherence to literal truth, but rather a weighing with the heart — the discipline of deed, and the unswerving reverence of the will.

All three of these elements should interweave, and in each it is only the "single" voice of love and freedom that can give the ultimate answers — a voice born of suffering and transformation. In this process, the need to search for new creative forms constantly arises, as well as for the revitalizing of archaic ones, in order to expand and develop language as a vessel for the spiritual reality; while on the other hand, there is the need to find anew its depths in simplicity. And here the redemption and rebirth of words become a reality which shines like a guiding star.

The above has been described in order to clarify the approach undertaken in making these translations. They are offered here in the hope that what has been received in the way of schooling and inner substance may, in gratitude, be reflected in some measure within them. There are assuredly many approaches to the art of translation. This is an attempt to illuminate and to share one of them.

Very fortunately it has been made possible to print here the original German text of the verses, together with the translations, in the first part of this volume.

As Rudolf Steiner's *Mystery Dramas* are undoubtedly his greatest poetic work, and as he referred to passages in them as containing impulses which can be helpful to poets of the future, they are a constant source of inspiration along the path just described. Therefore, and because of frequent requests for them, there are included here a number of the more poetic passages from my translation — begun in the 1940's — of his first three dramas.

And a still further group of translations has been added, translations which have arisen in response to varied artistic needs: for use on special occasions, for festivals, artistic programs, etc. — consisting of a number of prose passages from his books and lectures which seem to lie within the nature and scope of *Truth-Wrought-Words*. The first of these includes a translation of Rudolf Steiner's German rendering of the ancient Norwegian legend or folk song, *The Dream Song of Olaf Åsteson*. Details of its origin are described on page 120.

Also to be found in these pages are all the thought and help so generously given for the consummation and physical preparation of this book, for which I would like to express heartfelt gratitude, not only on my own behalf but on that of all who will now share here the fruits of these gifts and dedicated labors.

And finally, a word about the rendering of the title, "Wahrspruchworte." After years of pondering, two among many have seemed most possible. The one, "Heart-Truth-Words," reflects most nearly the sounds of the original, and holds validity in the sense of the quotation from *The Michael Letters* at the close of this volume. However, "Truth-Wrought-Words" has been chosen as being more revealing of the cosmic element creatively at work, which has wrought the original word-structures as vessels for its substance.

Arvia MacKaye Ege
Summer, 1977

From

Wahrspruchworte

TRUTH-WROUGHT-WORDS

ECCE HOMO

In dem Herzen webet Fühlen,
In dem Haupte leuchtet Denken,
In den Gliedern kraftet Wollen.

Webendes Leuchten,
Kraftendes Weben,
Leuchtendes Kraften:
Das ist der Mensch.

ECCE HOMO

In the heart the weaving feeling,
In the head the light of thinking,
In the limbs the strength of willing.
Weaving enlightening,
Strengthening weaving,
Enlightened strengthening:
Lo! This is man.

LICHT UND STERN

Es leuchten gleich Sternen
Am Himmel des ewigen Seins
Die gottgesandten Geister.
Gelingen mög' es allen Menschenseelen,
Im Reich des Erdenwerdens
Zu schauen ihrer Flammen Licht.

———

Zum Lichte uns zu wenden
In dunkler Zeiten Not,
Zum Geistesmorgenrot
Die Seelenblicke senden:
Menschenwollen sei es hier
Und bleib' es für und für.

1914

LIGHT AND STAR

They light up like stars
On the heaven of eternal being —
The god-inspired spirits.
Oh, may all human souls achieve,
In realms of earth-becoming,
The power to see their flaming light.

———

To turn us toward the light
In darkling times forlorn,
Toward Spirit's glowing morn
Direct the soul's clear sight:
Human willing be it — yea —
And be for aye and aye!

1914

BEIM LÄUTEN DER GLOCKEN

Das Schöne bewundern,
Das Wahre behüten,
Das Edle verehren,
Das Gute beschliessen:
Es führet den Menschen
Im Leben zu Zielen,
Im Handeln zum Rechten,
Im Fühlen zum Frieden,
Im Denken zum Lichte,
Und lehrt ihn vertrauen
Auf göttliches Walten
In Allem was ist:
Im Welten-All,
Im Seelengrund.

AT THE RINGING OF THE BELLS

To wonder at beauty,
Stand guard over truth,
Look up to the noble,
Decide for the good:
Leads man on his journey
To goals for his life,
To right in his doing,
To peace in his feeling,
To light in his thought,
And teaches him trust
In the guidance of God
In all that there is:
In the world-wide All,
In the soul's deep soil.

FINSTERNIS, LICHT, LIEBE

Dem Stoff sich verschreiben
Heisst Seelen zerreiben.

Im Geiste sich finden
Heisst Menschen verbinden.

Im Menschen sich schauen
Heisst Welten erbauen.

DARKNESS, LIGHT, LOVE

I

To bind oneself to matter
Means to grind the soul to dust.

To find oneself in spirit
Means to unite human beings.

To behold oneself in man
Means to build worlds.

II

Bind yourself to matter,
And souls as dust will scatter.

Find yourself in spirit,
And men are united within it.

See yourself in man,
And worlds are builded that gods began.

(Two renderings)

Uns ist gegeben
Auf keiner Stufe zu rasten.
Es leben, es streben die tätigen
Menschen von Leben zu Leben
Wie Pflanzen von Frühling
Zu Frühling — sich steigernd
Durch Irrtum zur Wahrheit hinauf,
Durch Fesseln zur Freiheit hinauf,
Durch Krankheit und Tod
Zu Schönheit, Gesundheit und Leben hinauf.

To us it is given
At no stage ever to rest.
They live and they strive the active
Human beings from life unto life
As plants grow from springtime
To springtime — ever aloft,
Through error upward to truth,
Through fetters upward to freedom,
Through illness and death
Upward to beauty, to health and to life.

(In response to Hölderlin's
Song of Destiny*)*

WELTENSEELENGEISTER

Im Lichte wir schalten,
Im Schauen wir walten,
Im Sinnen wir weben, —

Aus Herzen wir heben
Das Geistesringen
Durch Seelenschwingen;

Dem Menschen wir singen
Das Göttererleben
Im Weltengestalten.

WORLD-SOUL-SPIRITS

In light we are guiding,
In sight we are striding,
In musing we're weaving;

Out of hearts we're uprising
In spirit striving
On soul out-winging;

To man we are singing
Of the gods' exaltation
In world-all creation.

FRÜHLING

Der Sonnenstrahl,
Der lichterfunkelnde,
Er schwebt heran.

Die Blütenbraut,
Die farberregende,
Sie grüsst ihn froh.

Vertrauensvoll
Der Erdentochter
Erzählt der Strahl,

Wie Sonnenkräfte,
Die geistentsprossenen,
Im Götterheim
Dem Weltentone lauschen;

Die Blütenbraut,
Die farberglitzernde,
Sie höret sinnend
Des Lichtes Feuerton.

SPRING

The sun's bright beam,
The light-outsparkling one,
He hovers near.

The blossom-bride,
The color-wakening one,
She greets him glad.

Confiding in
The fair earth daughter,
The beam recounts

How sun-warm forces,
The spirit-springing ones,
In God's own home
List breathless to world music.

The blossom-bride,
The color-glistening one,
She harkens pondering
To the sunlight's fire-tone.

MICHAELS SCHWERT   Meteorisches Eisen

O Mensch,
Du bildest es zu deinem Dienste,
Du offenbarst es seinem Stoffeswerte nach
In vielen deiner Werke.
Es wird dir Heil jedoch erst sein,
Wenn dir sich offenbart
Seines Geistes Hochgewalt.

MICHAEL'S SWORD Meteoric Iron

    O Man,
You forge it daily to your use,
You reveal it in the value of its substance
In many of your works.
Yet it will only bring you healing
When it reveals to you
Its majestic spirit might.

MICHAEL-IMAGINATION

Sonnenmächten Entsprossene,
Leuchtende, Welten begnadende
Geistesmächte, zu Michaels Strahlenkleid
Seid ihr vorbestimmt vom Götterdenken.

Er, der Christusbote, weist in euch
Menschentragenden, heil'gen Welten-Willen;
Ihr, die hellen Ätherwelten-Wesen,
Trägt das Christuswort zum Menschen.

So erscheint der Christuskünder
Den erharrenden, durstenden Seelen;
Ihnen strahlet euer Leuchte-Wort
In des Geistesmenschen Weltenzeit.

Ihr, der Geist-Erkenntnis Schüler,
Nehmet Michaels weises Winken,
Nehmt des Welten-Willens Liebe-Wort
In der Seelen Höhenziele wirksam auf.

MICHAEL-IMAGINATION

Sun-all-mighty offspring,
Luminous, world-endowing
Spirit powers, to be Michael's garment of rays,
You are predestined by the thought of the gods.

He, the Christ proclaimer, makes manifest in you —
Mankind-sustainers — holy cosmic will;
You, the bright world-ether beings,
Bear the Christ's word to men.

So Christ's heralder appears
To longing, thirsting souls;
To them your word of light streams forth
In the cosmic era of spirit man.

You, the pupils of spirit knowledge,
Take Michael's wise, directing glance,
Take the World-Will's loving Word
Into your soul's high purpose, actively.

WEIHNACHT

Im Seelenaug' sich spiegelt
Der Welten Hoffnungslicht,
Dem Geist ergeb'ne Weisheit
Im Menschenherzen spricht:
Des Vaters ewige Liebe
Den Sohn der Erde sendet,
Der gnadevoll dem Menschenpfade
Die Himmelshelle spendet.

———

Offenbarung durch die Höhe dem Gotte,
Ruhe und Stille durch die Erdenräume,
Seligkeit in dem Menschen.

CHRISTMAS

The soul's clear eye reflects
The light of cosmic hope,
And spirit-devout wisdom
Speaks in human hearts;
The Father's eternal love
Sends forth His Son to earth,
Who sheds, with grace, upon man's path
The healing light of heaven.

———

Glory to God in the heights;
Peace and stillness through the earthly spaces;
Blessedness in mankind.

WINTERSONNENWENDE

Die Sonne schaue
Um mitternächtige Stunde.
Mit Steinen baue
Im leblosen Grunde.
So finde im Niedergang
Und in des Todes Nacht
Der Schöpfung neuen Anfang,
Des Morgens junge Macht.
Die Höhen lass offenbaren
Der Götter ewiges Wort;
Die Tiefen sollen bewahren
Den friedensvollen Hort.
Im Dunkel lebend
Erschaffe eine Sonne.
Im Stoffe webend
Erkenne Geistes Wonne.

CHRISTMAS

Behold the sun
At midnight hour,
And build with stones
In lifeless ground.
So find in downfall
And in death's dark night
Creation's new beginning,
The morning's youthful might.
The heights of heaven reveal
The gods' eternal Word;
The deeps shall guard and keep
Its gift of peace assured.
In darkness living
Create an inner sun.
In substance weaving
The spirit's joy is won.

Sterne sprachen einst zu Menschen,
Ihr Verstummen ist Weltenschicksal;
Des Verstummens Wahrnehmung
Kann Leid sein der Erdenmenschen;

In der stummen Stille aber reift,
Was Menschen sprechen zu Sternen;
Ihres Sprechens Wahrnehmung
Kann Kraft werden des Geistesmenschen.

Weihnachten, 1922

Stars spoke of old to men.
Their muteness is cosmic fate.
Perception of this muteness
Can quicken pain in earthly man.
Yet within the muted stillness ripens
What men speak to the stars.
Perception of this speech
Can quicken strength in spirit man.

Christmas, 1922

GEISTIGE KOMMUNION

Es nahet mir im Erdenwirken,
In Stoffes Abbild mir gegeben,
Der Sterne Himmelswesen:
Ich seh' im Wollen sie sich liebend wandeln.

Es dringen in mich im Wasserleben,
In Stoffes Kraftgewalt mich bildend,
Der Sterne Himmelstaten:
Ich seh' im Fühlen sie sich weise wandeln.

Sylvester, 1922-23

SPIRITUAL COMMUNION

There come to me in earth's activity,
In matter's image-imprint given me,
The stars' high-heaven-beings:
I see them lovingly transform themselves
                              in willing.

There permeate me in water's life,
In matter's forming-power creating me,
The stars' high-heaven-deeds:
I see them wisefully transform themselves
                              in feeling.

New Year, 1922-23

OSTERN

Steh' vor des Menschen Lebenspforte:
Schau an ihrer Stirne Weltenworte.

Leb' in des Menschen Seeleninnern:
Fühl in seinem Kreise Weltbeginnen.

Denk an des Menschen Erdenende:
Find' bei ihm die Geisteswende.

EASTER

Stand before man's great life-portal,
See upon its archway words immortal.

Live in man's own soul deep within,
Feel within its circuit how worlds begin.

Think upon man's earthly ending,
Find in it new spirit wending.

Weltentsprossenes Wesen, du in Lichtgestalt,
Von der Sonne erkraftet in der Mondgewalt,

Dich beschenket des Mars erschaffendes Klingen
Und Merkurs gliedbewegendes Schwingen,

Dich erleuchtet Jupiters erstrahlende Weisheit
Und der Venus liebetragende Schönheit —

Dass Saturns weltenalte Geist-Innigkeit
Dich dem Raumessein und Zeitenwerden weihe!

Ostern, 1924

Being sprung of the World-All — you, in stature of light,
From the Sun-orb empowered, in the Moon's pure might,

You are beshowered by Mars' form-fashioning ringing
And by Mercury's motion-swift quickening swinging,

You are illumined by Jupiter's wisdom out-streaming
And by Venus' love-bearing beauty out-beaming —

So that Saturn's age-old innermost spirit-embrace
May consecrate your entry into time and space!

Easter, 1924

"World-emburgeoned Being" is another possible translation for the beginning of the first line of this verse.

PFINGSTEN

Wo Sinneswissen endet,
Da stehet erst die Pforte,
Die Lebenswirklichkeiten
Dem Seelensein eröffnet,
Den Schlüssel schafft die Seele,
Wenn sie in sich erstarket
Im Kampf, den Weltenmächte
Auf ihrem eignen Grunde
Mit Menschenkräften führen,
Wenn sie durch sich vertreibt
Den Schlaf, der Wissenskräfte
An ihren Sinnesgrenzen
Mit Geistesnacht umhüllet.

———

Durch schwere Seelenhindernisse,
Durch wirre Geistesfinsternisse —
Zur ernsten Klarheit,
Zur lichten Wahrheit.

WHITSUN

Where sense perception ends,
There first is found the door
Which opens for the soul
True life realities.
The soul creates the key
When it grows strong within itself
In battle which world powers
Wage against human forces
Upon its own soul grounds;
When it dispels through its own strength
The sleep which, on the sill of sense,
Shrouds the powers of knowing
In spirit night.

———

Through tangling soul-hindrances,
Through wrangling spirit-darknesses,
To earnest clarity,
To shining verity.

TISCHGEBET

Es keimen die Pflanzen in der Erde Nacht,
Es sprossen die Kräuter durch der Luft Gewalt,
Es reifen die Früchte durch der Sonne Macht.

So keimet die Seele in des Herzens Schrein,
So sprosset des Geistes Macht im Licht der Welt,
So reifet des Menschen Kraft in Gottes Schein.

EIN GEHEIMNIS DER NATUR

Schaue die Pflanze!
Sie ist der von der Erde
Gefesselte Schmetterling.

Schaue den Schmetterling!
Er ist die vom Kosmos
Befreite Pflanze.

GRACE

The seeds are quickened in the night of the earth,
The young shoots spring in the power of the air,
The fruits grow ripe in the might of the sun.

So the soul is quickened in the heart's deep shrine,
So the might of the spirit springs in the light of the world,
So the power of man ripens in the glory of God.

―――

A SECRET OF NATURE

Behold the plant!
It is the butterfly
Held prisoner by the earth.

Behold the butterfly!
It is the plant
By the whole cosmos freed.

―――

Im Farbenschein des Äthermeeres
Gebiert des Lichtes webend Wesen
Der Menschenseele Geistgewebe;
Und geistbefruchtet reifend strebt
In Farbendunkels Raumestiefe
Hinaus die Lichtes-durst'ge Seele.
Bedürftig ist Natur des Geistes,
Der aus dem Seelensein ihr kraftet;
Bedürftig auch die Menschenseele
Der Kraft des Lichts im Weltenäther.

In the ether ocean's color shimmer
The weaving being of the light brings forth
The spirit web of the human soul.
And spirit fructified, the ripening
Light-thirsty soul strives outward
From spacial deeps of color darkness.
In need is nature of the spirit
Which flows to her from soul existence;
In need, also, the human soul
Of the powers of light in cosmic ether.

In der Lichtesluft des Geisterlandes
Da erblüh'n die Seelenrosen,
Und ihr Rot erstrahlet
In die Erdenschwere;
Es wird im Menschenwesen
Zum Herzgebild verdichtet:
Es strahlet in der Bluteskraft,
Als das Erdenrosenrot,
In die Geistesfelder wieder hin.

In the light-filled air of spirit lands
There the soul's red roses bloom,
And their red rays forth
Into the weight of earth;
Within man's being it becomes
Condensed into the organ of the heart;
And in the blood's life-force it rays,
As the deep rose-red of earth,
Back into the fields of spirit — once again.

DEN BERLINER FREUNDEN

Es siehet der Mensch
Mit dem welt-erzeugten Auge,
Ihn bindet, was er siehet
An Weltenfreude und Weltenschmerz,
Es bindet ihn an alles
Was da wird, aber minder nicht
An alles, was da stürzet
In Abgrundes finstre Reiche.

Es schaut der Mensch
Mit dem geistverliehnen Auge,
Ihn bindet, was er schauet
An Geisteshoffen und Geistes-Halte-Kraft,
Es bindet ihn an alles
Was in Ewigkeiten wurzelt
Und in Ewigkeiten Früchte trägt.

Aber schauen kann der Mensch
Nur wenn er des Innern Auge
Selber fühlet als Geistes-Gottes-Glied,
Das auf der Seele Schauplatz
Im Menschen-Leibes-Tempel
Der Götter Taten wirket.

TO THE BERLIN FRIENDS

Man looks out
With the world-engendered eye,
And what he sees thus binds him
To world delight and world despair.
It binds him unto all
That springs to life there, but not less
To all that plunges there
Into the dark abyss.

But man beholds
With the spirit-entrusted eye.
What he beholds thus binds him
To spirit hope and spirit's upholding power.
It binds him unto all
That roots within eternity
And bears within eternity its fruits.

Yet man can only then behold
When he feels the inner eye
Itself as God-given spirit organ,
Which at the focus of the soul,
Within the temple of man's body,
Fulfills the deeds of gods.

Es ist die Menschheit im Vergessen
An das Gottes-Innere.
Wir aber wollen es nehmen
In des Bewusstseins helles Licht
Und dann tragen über Schutt und Asche
Der Götter Flamme im Menschenherzen.

So mögen Blitze unsre Sinneshäuser
In Schutt zerschmettern:
Wir errichten Seelenhäuser
Auf der Erkenntnis
Eisenfestem Lichtesweben,
Und Untergang des Äussern
Soll werden Aufgang
Des Seelen-Innersten.

Das Leid dringet heran
Aus Stoffes-Kraft Gewalten,
Die Hoffnung leuchtet
Auch wenn Finsternis uns umwallt,
Und sie wird dereinst
In unsre Erinnerung dringen
Wenn wir nach der Finsternis
Im Lichte wieder leben dürfen.

Wir wollen nicht, dass diese Leuchte
Dereinst in künft'gen Helligkeiten uns fehle
Weil wir sie jetzt im Leide
Nicht in unsre Seelen eingepflanzet haben.

———

Mankind is in forgetfulness
Of the Godhead's innermost.
We, though, will raise it and take it
Into our consciousness, flooded with light
And then bear it over dust and ashes —
The divine flame in the human heart.

So may the lightning shatter into dust
Our sense-built houses.
We will erect instead soul houses
Built on knowledge,
Upon its iron-firm, light-woven web.
And downfall of the outer
Shall become uprise
Of the soul's own innermost.

For pain presses upon us
From powers of material force,
But hope illumines
Even when darkness enshrouds us,
And it will one day
Emerge within our memory
When at length, after the darkness,
We may live again in light.

We do not want this clear illumining
To be in future brightnesses denied us
Because we have not now,
In pain, implanted it within our souls.

Es bedarf der Mensch der innern Treue,
Der Treue zu der Führung der geistigen Wesen.
Er kann auf dieser Treue auferbauen
Sein ewiges Sein und Wesen,
Und das Sinnensein dadurch
Mit ewigem Licht
Durchströmen und durchkraften.

    Der Wolkendurchleuchter:
    Er durchleuchte,
    Er durchsonne,
    Er durchglühe,
    Er durchwärme
      Auch uns.*

The human soul has need of inward trust,
The trust in the guidance of spiritual beings.
For upon such trust she can erect
Her eternal life and being,
And sense-existence thus
Empower and imbue
With eternal light.

———

The Cloud-Illuminator —
May He fill with light,
May He flood with sun,
May He set aglow
And warm through and through
Even me.*

———

*May be used in either singular or plural.

GEBET FÜR KRANKE

O Gottesgeist erfülle mich,
Erfülle mich in meiner Seele;
Meiner Seele schenke starke Kraft,
Starke Kraft auch meinem Herzen,
Meinem Herzen, das dich sucht,
Das dich sucht durch tiefe Sehnsucht,
Tiefe Sehnsucht nach Gesundheit,
Nach Gesundheit und nach Starkmut,
Starkmut, der in meine Glieder strömt,
Strömt wie edles Gottgeschenk,
Gottgeschenk von dir, o Gottesgeist,
O Gottesgeist erfülle mich.

———

Ein Ich gab mir das Göttliche,
Die Menschheit weist mir Christus,
Die Seele wird mir der Geist beleben.

———

IN TIME OF ILLNESS

O Thou, God's Spirit, fill me full,
Fill me fully in my soul,
In my soul grant me strength,
Strength grant also to my heart,
To my heart that seeks to find thee,
Seeks to find thee through deep longing,
Through deep longing for well-being,
For well-being and strong courage,
Courage that through all my body streams,
Streams as noble gift of God,
Gift of God from Thee, O Thou, God's Spirit,
O Thou, God's Spirit, fill Thou me.

———

The Deity has given me my "I,"
The Christus shows me my humanity,
The Spirit will give my soul new life.

———

Des Menschen Kräfte sind zweifach geartet;
Es geht ein Strom von Kräften nach innen:
Er gibt Gehalt und inner Wurzelsein;
Es geht ein Strom von Kräften nach aussen:
Er gibt das Wohlsein und Lebenslichterhellung;
Drum denke sich als leichten Lichtmenschen,
Wen die Bildkräfte des schweren Körpermenschen plagen.

———

Die Kräfte sind leere Hülsen nur,
Entbehren sie den Geistgehalt,
Doch sind sie Schöpferwirksamkeiten,
Wenn sie den Geist umkleiden.

———

The forces of man are dual in nature.
One stream of forces takes its way inward:
This one gives content and inner root-being;
One stream of forces takes its way outward:
This gives well-being and life-freshening light.
Think yourself therefore as a weightless light-man
Plagued by the form-force of his weighted body.

―――

All forces are but empty husks
When destitute of spirit content;
But they are strong creative powers
When they clothe the spirit.

―――

Es keimen der Seele Wünsche,
Es wachsen des Willens Taten,
Es reifen des Lebens Früchte.

Ich fühle mein Schicksal,
Mein Schicksal findet mich.
Ich fühle meinen Stern,
Mein Stern findet mich.
Ich fühle meine Ziele,
Meine Ziele finden mich.

Meine Seele und die Welt sind eines nur.

Das Leben, es wird heller um mich,
Das Leben, es wird schwerer für mich,
Das Leben, es wird reicher in mir.

The soul's questings are quickening.
The will's deeds are waxing.
And life's fruits grow ripe.

I feel my destiny,
My destiny finds me.
I feel my star,
My star finds me.
I feel my goals,
My goals find me.

My soul and the world are but one.

Life becomes brighter about me.
Life becomes harder for me.
Life becomes richer within me.

Wenn der Mensch, warm in Liebe,
Sich der Welt als Seele gibt,
Wenn der Mensch, licht im Sinnen,
Von der Welt den Geist erwirbt,
Wird in Geist-erhellter Seele,
Wird in Seele-getragenem Geist,
Der Geistesmensch im Leibesmenschen
Sich wahrhaft offenbaren.

When in warmth of love
Man gives himself as soul unto the world,
When in light of contemplation
Man wins the spirit from the world,
Then in spirit-lumined soul,
Then in soul-supported spirit,
Will spirit man in earthly man
Be verily revealed.

Suche im eignen Wesen
Und du findest die Welt;
Suche im Weltenwalten
Und du findest dich selbst;
Merke den Pendelschlag
Zwischen Selbst und Welt:
Und dir offenbart sich
Menschen-Welten-Wesen;
Welten-Menschen-Wesen.

Seek in your own being
And you will find the world;
Seek in world wide being
And you will find yourself;
Note the constant swing
Between self and world
And you will find revealed:
The human-cosmic-being;
The cosmic-human-being.

Sonne, du strahlentragende,
Deines Lichtes Stoffgewalt
Zaubert Leben aus der Erde
Unermesslich reichen Tiefen.

Herz, du seelentragendes,
Deines Lichtes Geistgewalt
Zaubert Leben aus der Menschen
Unermesslich tiefem Innern.

Schaue ich in die Sonne,
Spricht ihr Licht mir strahlend
Von dem Geist, der gnadevoll
Durch Weltenwesen wandelt.

Fühl' ich in mein Herz,
Spricht der Geist sein Eigenwort,
Von dem Menschen, den er liebt
Durch alle Zeit und Ewigkeit.

Sehen kann ich aufwärtsblickend
In der Sonne hellem Rund
Das gewalt'ge Weltenherz.

Fühlen kann ich einwärtsschauend
In des Herzens warmem Schlag
Die beseelte Menschensonne.

Sun, you radiance-harborer,
Your pure light's material power
Conjures life from out the earth's
Immeasurably fertile deeps.

Heart, you soul-source-harborer,
Your warm light's bright spirit power
Conjures life from out man's own
Immeasurably deep inmost.

When I gaze into the sun,
Radiantly it speaks to me
Of the spirit who, grace-giving,
Wends throughout the world-all-being.

When I feel into my heart,
The spirit speaks its own true word —
Speaks of man, he whom it loves
Through time and all eternity.

I can see, when I look upward
Deep into the sun's bright orb,
The world's great glowing heart.

I can feel, when I look inward
Deep into the heart's warm beat,
The soul-bright human sun.

Ich schaue in die Finsternis.
In ihr erstehet Licht,
Lebendes Licht.
Wer ist dies Licht in der Finsternis?
Ich bin es selbst in meiner Wirklichkeit.
Diese Wirklichkeit des Ich
Tritt nicht ein in mein Erdensein,
Ich bin nur Bild davon.
Ich werde es aber wiederfinden
Wenn ich guten Willens für den Geist
Durch des Todes Pforte geschritten.

———

Strahlender als die Sonne,
reiner als der Schnee,
feiner als der Äther
ist das Selbst,
der Geist in meinem Herzen.
Dies Selbst bin ich — ich bin dies Selbst.

I gaze into the darkness.
In it arises light,
Living light.
Who is this light in the darkness?
It is I myself in my reality!
This reality of "I"
Does not enter here my earth existence.
I am but image of it.
But I shall find it once again
When I, with good will for the spirit,
Have passed through the gate of death.

———

More radiant than the sun,
Purer than the snow,
Finer than the ether
Is the Self,
The spirit in my heart.
This Self am I — I am this Self.

Es muss sein Sondersein und Leben opfern,
wer Geistesziele schauen will
durch Sinnesoffenbarung;
wer sich erkühnen will,
in seinen Eigenwillen
den Geisteswillen zu ergiessen.

———

Der Mensch findet
Des Ewigen Grund,
Wenn er, mit vollem Vertrauen,
In seines Wesens Tiefen ahnet
Des Gottes Werk.

———

He must give up his separate life and being
Who would behold the spirit's goals
Through sense's revelation;
Who would make bold to pour
Into his personal will
The spirit-will's high power.

———

Man finds
His eternal ground
When he, in full trust,
Breathes within his depths
The work of God.

———

TINTAGEL

Von vielsagenden Burgestrümmern kommen wir.
Hier sassen einst die alten Dämonenbesieger,
Verstärkend des Führers Kraft durch die Sternenzwölf.
Die Burgen sind in Trümmern,
Die Astralwelt ist verstummt:
Doch Geisterkraft wuchtet um den Berg,
Und Seelenbildemacht stürmt vom Meer ...
Zaubrisch wechselnd sind Licht- und Lüfteringen,
Die kräftig zu der Seele dringen
Auch heute nach dreitausend Jahren,
Neu und aus der Elemente Erinnerungsbildern ...

(Aus einem Brief an Albert Steffen, 1924)

Aus Gottessein erstand die Menschenseele,
Sie kann in Wesensgrunde sterbend tauchen,
Sie wird dem Tod dereinst den Geist entbinden.

TINTAGEL

We come from old impressive ruined castles.
Here sat of old the ancient demon-conquerors,
Strengthening their leader's power through the starry twelve.
The castles are in ruins;
The astral world is mute.
Yet spirit power still thrives about the cliffs
And powerful soul-pictures storm up from the sea ...
Magically interchanging is the interplay of light and air
That presses forcefully upon the soul,
Even today, after three thousand years,
Anew, and out of the memory pictures of the elements ...

(From a letter to Albert Steffen, 1924)

From out the Godhead sprang the human soul
And dying can dive down to depths of being;
It will one day from all death set the spirit free.

Es wollte im Sinnenstoffe
Das Goetheanum vom Ewigen
In Formen zum Auge sprechen:
Die Flammen konnten den Stoff verzehren.
Es soll die Anthroposophie
Aus Geistigem ihren Bau
Zur Seele sprechen lassen:
Die Flammen des Geistes
Sie werden sie erhärten.

———

Erkennt der Mensch sich selbst:
Wird ihm das Selbst zur Welt;
Erkennt der Mensch die Welt:
Wird ihm die Welt zum Selbst.

———

The Goetheanum wanted
To speak of the eternal
To the eye, in form-wrought substance.
The substance could be consumed by fire.
But Anthroposophy
Would let its form-wrought building speak
To the soul, out of the spirit.
The fire of the spirit
Will harden and affirm it.

———

If man fully knows himself:
His self becomes the world;
If man fully knows the world:
The world becomes his self.

———

Aus des Geistes lichten Höhen
Erstrahle Gottes helles Licht
In Menschenseelen
Die suchen wollen
Des Geistes Gnade
Des Geistes Kraft
Des Geistes Sein.

Er lebe
Im Herzen,
Im Seelen-Innern
Unserer
Die wir
In Seinem Namen
Hier uns versammelt fühlen.

Out of the Spirit's luminous heights,
May there stream God's clear, pure light
Into human souls
Who will to seek
The Spirit's grace,
The Spirit's power,
The Spirit's being.
May He live
In these hearts,
These inmost souls
Of ours,
As we,
In His Name,
Feel ourselves united here.

Es offenbart die Weltenseele sich
Am Kreuze des Weltenleibes.
Sie lebet fünfstrahlig leuchtend
Durch Weisheit, Liebe, Willenskraft,
Durch Allsinn und durch Ichsinn
Und findet so
Den Geist der Welt in sich.

———

Aus dem Geiste ist alles Sein entsprungen,
In dem Geiste wurzelt alles Leben,
Nach dem Geiste zielen alle Wesen.

The soul of the world lies out-stretched
Upon the cross of the world's body.
In five out-beaming rays, luminously, it lives
Through wisdom, love, and power of will,
Through all-awareness and ego-awareness,
Finding thus
Within itself the Spirit of the World.

———

Out of the Spirit all being has sprung;
In the Spirit all life is rooted;
Toward the Spirit all beings are striving.

Ich möchte jeden Menschen
Aus des Kosmos' Geist entzünden,
Dass er Flamme werde
Und feurig seines Wesens
Wesen entfalte.

Die Andern, sie möchten
Aus des Kosmos' Wasser nehmen,
Was die Flammen verlösche
Und wäss'rig alles Wesen
Im Innern lähmt.

O Freude, wenn die Menschenflamme
Lodert auch da wo sie ruht!
O Bitternis, wenn das Menschending
Gebunden wird da, wo es regsam sein möchte.

I would enkindle every man
From out the spirit of the cosmos
That he become a flame,
And unfold in fire
His being's very nature.

The others, they would take,
Out of the cosmos, water,
To quench with it the flames;
And dampening all being,
Lame it from within.

Oh joy, when the human flame
Is aglow, even there where it rests;
Oh bitterness, when the human thing
Is bound there, where it longs to be active.

VERSES

FOR CHILDREN

ABENDGEBET FÜR KINDER

Vom Kopf bis zum Fuss
Bin ich Gottes Bild,
Vom Herzen bis in die Hände
Fühl ich Gottes Hauch,
Sprech ich mit dem Munde,
Folg ich Gottes Willen.
Wenn ich Gott erblicke
Überall,
In Vater und Mutter,
In allen lieben Menschen,
In Tier und Blume,
In Baum und Stein,
Gibt Furcht mir nichts,
Nur Liebe
Zu allem was um mich ist.

CHILD'S EVENING PRAYER

From my head to my feet
I'm the picture of God;
From my heart into my hands
I feel God's living breath.
When I speak with my mouth,
I follow God's own will.
When I gaze on God
In the whole world-all,
In father and mother,
In all dear people,
In beast and flower,
In tree and stone,
No fear can come near,
Only love —
For all that's around me here.

MORGENSPRUCH

Für die vier unteren Klassen

Der Sonne liebes Licht,
Es hellet mir den Tag;
Der Seele Geistesmacht,
Sie gibt den Gliedern Kraft;
Im Sonnen-Lichtes-Glanz
Verehre ich, o Gott,
Die Menschenkraft, die Du
In meine Seele mir
So gütig hast gepflanzt,
Dass ich kann arbeitsam
Und lernbegierig sein.
Von Dir stammt Licht und Kraft,
Zu Dir ström' Lieb' und Dank.

September 26, 1919

MORNING VERSE

For grades one through four

The sun with loving light
Makes bright for me the day.
The soul with spirit power
Gives strength unto my limbs.
In sunlight's radiant glance
I reverence, O God,
The human power which you
So lovingly have planted
For me within my soul,
That I with all my might
May love to work and learn.
From you come light and strength;
To you stream love and thanks.

September 26, 1919

MORGENSPRUCH
Für die oberen Klassen

Ich schaue in die Welt,
In der die Sonne leuchtet,
In der die Steine funkeln,
In der die Steine lagern;
Die Pflanzen lebend wachsen,
Die Tiere fühlend leben,
In der der Mensch beseelt,
Dem Geiste Wohnung gibt;

Ich schaue in die Seele,
Die mir im Innern lebet.
Der Gottesgeist, er webt
Im Sonn' — und Seelenlicht,
Im Weltenraum, da draussen,
In Seelentiefen, drinnen. —

Zu Dir, o Gottesgeist,
Will bittend ich mich wenden,
Dass Kraft und Segen mir
Zum Lernen und zur Arbeit
In meinem Innern wachse.

September 26, 1919

MORNING VERSE
For grades five through twelve

I look into the world
In which the sun is shining,
In which the stars are sparkling,
In which the stones repose;
Where living plants are growing,
Where sentient beasts are living,
Where man, soul-gifted, gives
The spirit a dwelling place.

I look into the soul
That lives within my being.
The World-Creator moves
In sunlight and in soul-light,
In wide world space without,
In soul-depths here within.

To Thee, Creator-Spirit,
I will now turn my heart
To beg that strength and blessing
To learn and work may grow
Within my inmost being.

September 26, 1919

VERSES

FOR THE DEAD

FÜR DIE TOTEN

Geister eurer Seelen, wirkende Wächter,
Eure Schwingen mögen bringen
Unserer Seelen bittende Liebe
Eurer Hut vertrauten Sphärenmenschen.
Dass, mit eurer Macht geeint,
Unsere Bitte helfend strahle
Den Seelen, die sie liebend sucht.

———

Die Ihr wachet über Sphärenseelen,
Die Ihr webet an den Sphärenseelen,
Geister, die Ihr über Seelenmenschen schützend
Aus der Weltenweisheit liebend wirkt —
Höret unsere Bitte,
Schauet unsere Liebe,
Die mit Euren helfenden Kräfteströmen
Sich einen möchten,
Geist-erahnend, Liebe-strahlend.

FOR THE DEAD

Spirits of your souls, great active guardians,
May your swinging pinions bring
Our souls' entreating love
To the human beings of the spheres
Entrusted to your care;
That united with your power
Our entreaty stream with help
To the souls whom lovingly we seek.

———

You, who watch over the souls of the spheres,
You, who waft about the souls of the spheres,
Spirits, who, working out of cosmic wisdom,
Lovingly protect soul-human-beings —
Hear our request,
Behold our love,
Who seek to unite ourselves with the outpouring
Of your helping forces,
Spirit-perceiving, love-out-streaming.

Meine Liebe sei den Hüllen,
Die dich jetzt umgeben,
Kühlend deine Hitze,
Wärmend deine Kälte,
Opfernd einverwoben.
Lebe liebgetragen,
Lichtbeschenkt nach oben.

———

Im Lichte der Weltgedanken,
Da webet die Seele, die
Vereint mit mir auf Erden.

*

Meines Herzens warmes Leben,
Es ströme zu deiner Seele hin,
Zu wärmen deine Kälte,
Zu sänftigen deine Hitze.
In den Geisteswelten
Mögen leben meine Gedanken in deinen,
Und deine Gedanken in meinen.

May my love be interwoven,
As my heart's offering,
In the sheaths that now surround you,
Cooling all your heat,
Warming all your cold.
Live — love-upborne,
Light-rayed-through — on upward.

———

In the light of world-all thoughts,
There weaves the soul, who
Was united with me on earth.
*
The warm life of my heart
Flows out to your soul,
To warm your cold,
To soothe your heat.
In the spirit worlds
May my thoughts live within thine,
And your thoughts within mine.

Es strebe zu dir meiner Seele Liebe,
Es ströme zu dir meiner Liebe Sinn.
Sie mögen dich tragen,
Sie mögen dich halten
In Hoffnungshöhen,
In Liebessphären.

———

In Geistgefilde will ich senden
Die treue Liebe, die wir fanden,
Um Seele mit der Seele zu verbinden.
Du sollst mein Denken liebend finden
Wenn aus des Geistes lichten Landen
Du suchend wirst die Seele wenden,
Zu schauen, was in mir du suchest.

The love of my soul
Is striving to you.
My love's pure sensing
Is streaming to you.
May they bear you aloft
And uphold you there,
In hope's wide heights,
In love's clear spheres.

———

Into spirit pastures I will send
The faithful love which here we found
That we might be united soul with soul.
So may you find my thinking ever loving
When from the spirit's light-filled lands
You, searching, turn your gaze of soul
To see what here in me you seek.

DER TOTE SPRICHT

Im Leuchtenden,
Da fühle ich
Die Lebenskraft.
Der Tod hat mich
Vom Schlaf erweckt,
Vom Geistesschlaf.

Ich werde sein,
Und aus mir tun,
Was Leuchtekraft
In mir erstrahlt.

THE ONE WHO HAS DIED SPEAKS

In radiant light
'Tis there I feel
The power of life.
For death
Has wakened me from sleep —
From spirit sleep.

Oh, I shall be
And do from out me
What radiant power
Within me shines.

Ich war mit euch vereint,
Bleibet in mir vereint.
Wir werden zusammen sprechen
In der Sprache des ewigen Seins.
Wir werden tätig sein
Da wo der Taten Ergebnis wirkt.
Wir werden weben im Geiste,
Da wo gewoben werden Menschen-Gedanken,
Im Wort des ew'gen Gedanken.

I was united with you,
So remain united in me.
Together we shall speak
The speech of eternal being.
Together we shall act
Where the results of the deeds are at work.
Together we shall weave in spirit,
Where human thought is woven,
In the Word of eternal thought.

THE

FOUNDATION STONE

Two Renderings

Menschenseele!
Du lebest in den Gliedern,
Die dich durch die Raumeswelt
In das Geistesmeereswesen tragen:
Übe *Geist-Erinnern*
In Seelentiefen,
Wo in waltendem
Weltenschöpfer-Sein
Das eigne Ich
Im Gottes-Ich
Erweset,
Und du wirst wahrhaft leben
Im Menschen-Welten-Wesen.

Denn es waltet der Vater-Geist der Höhen
In den Weltentiefen Sein-erzeugend:
Ihr Kräfte-Geister,
Lasset aus den Höhen erklingen,
Was in den Tiefen das Echo findet,
Dieses spricht:
Aus dem Göttlichen weset die Menschheit.

Das hören die Geister in Ost, West, Nord, Süd:
Menschen mögen es hören.

Soul of Man!
Thou livest in the limbs,
Which bear thee through the world of space
Into the ocean of spirit being:
Practice *spirit-recalling*
In depths of soul,
Where in empowering
World-Creator-Being
Thine inmost I
In God's own I
Takes being,
And thou shalt truly *live*
In human world-all being.

For the Father-Spirit of the heights reigns
In the depths of the world, begetting being;
Ye Spirits of Strength,
Let out of the heights ring forth
What in the depths finds there its echo,
Speaking thus:
Out of the Godhead is created mankind.

This is heard by the Spirits in East, West, North, South;
May human beings hear it!

Menschenseele!
Du lebest in dem Herzens-Lungen-Schlage,
Der dich durch den Zeitenrhythmus
Ins eigne Seelenwesensfühlen leitet:
Übe *Geist-Besinnen*
Im Seelengleichgewichte,
Wo die wogenden
Welten-Werde-Taten
Das eigene Ich
Dem Welten-Ich
Vereinen,
Und du wirst wahrhaft fühlen
Im Menschen-Seelen-Wirken.

Denn es waltet der Christus-Wille im Umkreis
In den Weltenrhythmen Seelen-begnadend:
Ihr Lichtes-Geister,
Lasset vom Osten befeuern,
Was durch den Westen sich formet,
Dieses spricht:
In dem Christus wird Leben der Tod.

Das hören die Geister in Ost, West, Nord, Süd:
Menschen mögen es hören.

Soul of Man!
Thou livest in the pulse of heart and lung,
Which leadeth thee through the rhythm of time
Into the feeling of thine own soul being:
Practice *spirit-communing*
In the soul's fine balance,
Where the on-surging,
World-Evolving-Deeds
Thine inmost I
With the World's own I
Unite,
And thou shalt truly *feel*
In human soul inner-working.

For the Christ-Will reigns in the spheres encircling us
In the rhythms of the world, shedding grace upon souls;
Ye Spirits of Light,
Let from the East be enkindled
What through the West takes on form,
Speaking thus:
In Christ death becomes life.

This is heard by the Spirits in East, West, North, South;
May human beings hear it!

Menschenseele!
Du lebest im ruhenden Haupte,
Das dir aus Ewigkeitsgründen
Die Weltgedanken erschliesset:
Übe *Geist-Erschauen*
In Gedanken-Ruhe,
Wo die ew'gen Götterziele
Welten-Wesens-Licht
Dem eignen Ich
Zu freiem Wollen
Schenken,
Und du wirst wahrhaft denken
In Menschen-Geistes-Gründen.

Denn es walten des Geistes Weltgedanken
Im Weltenwesen Licht-erflehend:
Ihr Seelen-Geister,
Lasset aus den Tiefen erbitten,
Was in den Höhen erhöret wird,
Dieses spricht:
In des Geistes Weltgedanken erwachet die Seele.

Das hören die Geister in Ost, West, Nord, Süd:
Menschen mögen es hören.

Soul of Man!
Thou livest in the quiet of the head,
Which from out eternal foundations
Lays open unto thee the world-all thoughts:
Practice *spirit-beholding*
In thought, stilled through,
Where the eternal aims of the gods
Cosmic-Beings'-Light
On thine inmost I
For thy free willing
Are shedding,
And thou shalt truly *think*
In human spirit foundations.

For the Spirit's World-All Thoughts reign
In the being of the world, light-beseeching;
Ye Spirits of Soul,
Let out of the deeps be entreated
What in the heights may be heard,
Speaking thus:
In the Spirit's World-All Thoughts the soul awakens.

This is heard by the Spirits in East, West, North, South;
May human beings hear it!

In der Zeiten Wende
Trat das Welten-Geistes-Licht
In den irdischen Wesensstrom;
Nacht-Dunkel
Hatte ausgewaltet;
Taghelles Licht
Erstrahlte in Menschenseelen;
Licht,
Das erwärmet
Die armen Hirtenherzen;
Licht,
Das erleuchtet
Die weisen Königshäupter.

Göttliches Licht,
Christus-Sonne
Erwärme
Unsere Herzen,
Erleuchte
Unsere Häupter,
Dass gut werde,
Was wir
Aus Herzen gründen,
Was wir
Aus Häuptern
Zielvoll führen wollen.

At the turn of time
Cosmic-Spirit-Light descended
Into earthly stream of being;
Darkling night
Had run its course;
Day-clear light
Streamed into human souls;
Light
That enwarms
The humble shepherds' hearts;
Light
That enlightens
The wise heads of kings.

God-given light,
Christus-Sun,
Enwarm
For us our hearts,
Enlighten
For us our heads,
That good may be
What we
From our hearts do found,
What we
From our heads
Direct with single will.

Rendering number I was completed in 1978. In verse 3, on page 105, the translation "World-All" is preferred, but "Cosmic" may also be used as an alternative.

Rendering number II was worked on together with Dr. Hermann Poppelbaum during the Second World War.

II.

Soul of Man!
Thou livest in the limbs
Which bear thee through the realms of space
Into the ocean of spirit-being:
Oh, *recall the spirit*
In depths of soul
Where in the power
Of World-Creator-Being
Thy self
Taketh being
From Self-Divine,
And thou shalt truly *live*
In human cosmic being.

For the Father-Spirit of the heights reigns
In the depths of the world, begetting being;
Ye Spirits of Strength,
Let from the heights ring forth
What in the deeps its echo findeth,
Speaking thus:
From the Divine springeth mankind.

Spirit beings hear it in East, West, North, South;
May human beings hear it!

Soul of Man!
Thou livest in the pulse of heart and lung
Which leadeth thee through the rhythm of time
Into the feeling of thine own soul being:
Oh, *bethink the spirit*
In soul's equilibrium
Where the up-surging,
World-evolving deeds
Unite
Thy very self
With Cosmic Selfhood,
And thou shalt truly *feel*
In human soul-life's action.

For the Christ-Will reigns, encircling us
In the rhythms of the world, blessing all souls;
Ye Spirits of Light,
Let from the East be enkindled
What through the West is being formed,
Speaking thus:
In Christ death takes on life.

Spirit beings hear it in East, West, North, South;
May human beings hear it!

Soul of Man!
Thou livest in stillness of head
Which from foundations eternal
Unsealeth for thee thought universal:
Oh, *behold the spirit*
When thy thoughts are stilled,
Where eternal aims divine
Grant Cosmic-Beings'-Light
To thine own self
To use
In thy free willing,
And thou shalt truly *think*
Where human spirit is rooted.

For the Cosmic Thoughts of the Spirit reign
In cosmic being, light beseeching;
Ye Spirits of Soul,
Let from the deeps be entreated
What in the heights shall be heard,
Speaking thus:
In the Spirit's Cosmic Thoughts the soul awaketh.

Spirit beings hear it in East, West, North, South;
May human beings hear it!

From

THE MYSTERY DRAMAS

Poetic Excerpts

These excerpts from Rudolf Steiner's first three Mystery Dramas are included in this volume of his verses as, in most cases, their whole form, content and character places them in a particular way in the poetic sphere. A few, however, have been chosen more from the aspect of the quality of their content, through which, as entities in themselves, they offer special spiritual nourishment, although in form their poetic character may seem less pronounced.

Among the former are the speeches of: The Soul Forces: Philia, Astrid, Luna and the Other Philia; Lucifer and Ahriman; Benedictus; Spirit Voice, or the Voice of Conscience; and the Fairy Tales told by Dame Balde. The latter include speeches by: Theodora, Maria, Johannes and others.

The translation attempts throughout to adhere as closely as possible to the poetic form, rhythm and sounds of the original German, as well as to the meaning.

A description of the settings of the various scenes has been indicated in order to give the surroundings within which the words are spoken, as well as to aid the reader in following the thread of continuity throughout the course of the action, as what appears here can give only a fragmentary aspect of the whole.

Those who are not yet familiar with the dramas will, it is hoped, through reading these excerpts, be moved to make a study of the plays in full.

From
THE PORTAL OF INITIATION

(From the Prologue)

The light of the sun is flooding
The realms of space,
The song of the birds reechoes
Through the fields of the air,
The blessing of plants springs forth
From the being of the earth,
And human souls rise up
With grateful hearts
To join the spirits of the world.

———

(From Scene I)

A room, rose-red in tone, adjoining a lecture hall. Various persons enter and talk together of the lecture they have just heard.
(Words spoken by Maria and Theodora during the scene are quoted as fragments.)

MARIA: When the words of many human beings
Present themselves before the soul as now,
It is as if
Amid them stood, mysteriously,
The Archetype of Man.
It shows itself diversified in many souls,
Just as the single light
Within the rainbow's arch
Reveals itself in many-colored hues.

———

(Later in the scene)

THEODORA:
    I am impelled to speak.
    Before my spirit stands a Form in shining light;
    And from it words sound forth to me.
    I feel myself in future times,
    And human beings I perceive
    Who are not yet alive.
    They also see the Form.
    They also hear the words.
    'T is so they sound:
    You have lived long in faith,
    You have been comforted by hope,
    So now be comforted with sight,
    Be quickened now through Me.
    I lived within the souls
    Who sought Me in themselves,
    Through My own servants' words,
    Through their devotions' power.
    You have beheld the senses' light,
    Have had to put your faith in spirit realms;
    But now you have achieved
    A drop of worthy seership.
    Oh feel it deeply in your souls.

— — — — — — — — — — —

    A human being
    Emerges from this radiant light.
    It speaks to me:
    You shall proclaim to all
    Of those who wish to hear you

That you have seen
What men shall soon experience.
The Christ once lived upon the earth,
And from this life it follows
That He encircles in soul form
All growth of man.
He is united with the spirit part of earth.
But human beings could not yet behold Him
As He reveals Himself in such existence,
Because their beings lacked the eyes of spirit
Which shall in future show themselves.
But near is now the future
When with new powers of sight
The men on earth shall be endowed.
What once the senses saw
When Christ trod on the earth
Shall souls of men one day behold,
When soon the time shall be fulfilled.

(From Scene III)

A Meditation Room

BENEDICTUS:
>   The weaving essence of the light streams forth
>   Through far-flung spaces
>   To fill all the world with life.
>
>   The grace of love pours forth its warmth
>   Through time's long ages
>   To call forth the revelation of all worlds.
>
>   And spirit messengers, they wed
>   The weaving essence of the light
>   With soul-world revelation;
>
>   And when with both the human being
>   Can wed his own true self,
>   He is alive in spirit heights.

———

SPIRIT VOICE behind the scenes:
>   His thoughts are now descending
>   To world foundations;
>   What as shadow he has thought,
>   What as phantom he has lived,
>   Is freed now from the world of form,
>   From out whose fullness
>   All men, bethinking,
>   In shadow dream;
>   From out whose fullness
>   All men, beholding,
>   In phantom dwell.

———

(From Scene IV)

A landscape, the unique nature of which expresses the character of the Soul World.

LUCIFER: O man, know thou thyself;
O man, feel thou me.
Thou hast freed thyself
From spirit guidance,
Hast taken refuge
In free earth realms.
Thou soughtst thine own true being
In earth confusion;
To find thyself
Was thy reward,
Thy destiny.
Thou foundest me.
The spirits wished
To lay a veil before thy senses.
I tore the veil in two.
The spirits wished
To follow their own will in thee.
I gave thee thine own will.
O man, know thou thyself;
O man, feel thou me.

AHRIMAN: O man, know thou me;
O man, feel thou thyself.
Thou hast escaped
From spirit darkness.
Thou hast attained
The light of earth.
So suck the power of truth
From my solidity.
I harden stable ground.

          The spirits wished
          To wrest from thee the senses' beauty.
          I activate this beauty
          In solid light.
          I carry thee
          Into essential being.
          O man, know thou me;
          O man, feel thou thyself.

LUCIFER: There was no time
          When thou didst not feel me.
          I've followed thee throughout life courses.
          I was allowed to fill thee
          With powerful strength of selfhood,
          Self-being's joy.

AHRIMAN: There was no time
          When thou didst not behold me.
          Thy senses' eyes have looked upon me
          Through all earth evolution.
          I was allowed to shine for thee
          In stately beauty,
          In revelation's blissfulness.

JOHANNES: *(to himself, in meditation)*
          This is the sign about which Benedictus spoke.
          Two great powers stand before the world of soul.
          The one dwells deep within us as the tempter,
          The other dulls the gaze
          When it is focused toward without.
          The one assumed but now the woman's form
          Who brought before my eye the soul's delusion.
          The other can be found in everything.

(From Scene V)

A SUBTERRANEAN ROCK TEMPLE

BENEDICTUS:

> *(in the East)*
> As you have been my true companions
> In realms of everlasting life,
> So I am come within your midst
> Today, to ask the help
> I need from you to weave
> The threads of destiny for one
> Who must receive through us the light.
> Through many trials and sorrows he has passed
> And has in bitter pain of soul
> Laid ground for consecration
> Which now shall bring him knowledge.
> My task is thus fulfilled
> As spirit-messenger, to bring
> The treasures of this temple
> To earthly human beings.
> It lies with you, my brothers, now
> To carry out my work.
> I have revealed to him the light
> Which guided him
> To his first spirit vision.
> But shall the truth
> Be born of image,
> So must your work
> Be added unto mine.
> My word springs forth from me alone.
> Through you the cosmic spirits sound.

THEODOSIUS:
> *(in the South)*
> Here speaks the power of love,
> Uniting worlds
> And filling beings with existence.
> Let warmth now flow into his heart;
> And he shall realize
> He nears the cosmic spirit
> By giving up the vain illusion
> Of his self-bound life.
> You have at last set free
> His sight from sleep of sense;
> Now warmth shall stir and wake the spirit
> From out his soul's deep being.
> You have drawn forth the self
> From out his body's sheath;
> Now love shall make his soul grow firm,
> That so it may become a mirror
> Wherein must be perceived
> What happens in the spirit world.
> For love will give to him the power
> To feel himself as spirit,
> And so create for him the ear
> To hear the spirit speech.

ROMANUS: *(in the West)*
> My words are also not
> The revelation of my being;
> Through me the world-will speaks.
> And as you have so strengthened
> The one entrusted to your care
> With power to live in spirit,

So shall this power lead him
Beyond the bounds of space and ends of time.
Into those spheres he now shall pass
Where spirits act, creative.
They will reveal themselves to him,
Demanding of him deeds.
He will fulfill them gladly.
The cosmic builders' goals
Shall quicken him with life;
Divine primordial sources
Bespirit him;
The world-indwelling warriors
Empower him;
The sphere-bright lordlings
Enlighten him;
And cosmic rulers
Befire him.

(From Scene VI)

The same setting as Scene IV.

(In the presence of the Spirit of the Elements, Dame Balde tells a fairy tale.)

DAME BALDE:
    There was one time a being
    Who flew from east to west
    Following the sun.
    It flew on over land and over sea;
    And from the heights it watched
    The busy life of men.
    It saw how human beings love
    And how they hate each other.
    And there was naught could hinder
    This being in its flight.
    For hate and love create
    Always the same a thousandfold.
    Yet o'er a certain house
    The being had to pause.
    Within there was a tired man
    Who pondered over human love
    And pondered, too, on human hate.
    And all his pondering
    Had carved deep furrows in his face,
    Had turned his hair quite white.
    Absorbed in his deep sorrow,
    The being lost its sun-bright guide
    And stayed with the old man.
    It was still in his room
    After the sun had long gone down;
    And when the sun arose again,

The being was once more
Caught upward by the great sun-spirit.
Once more it saw the people
In love and hate
Upon their earthly course.
And when it came a second time
Above the house, in its sun-journeying,
Its earthward gaze
Beheld a dead man there.

(From Scene VII)

THE SPIRIT REALM

(Maria and the Three Soul Forces)

MARIA: You, my sisters, who have
So often been my helpers,
Be so once more in this same hour
That I may make world ether
Resound within itself,
Ring out in harmony,
And ringing fill a soul
To brimming with clear knowing.
I can behold the signs
That lead us to our task.
So shall your work, my sisters,
Unite itself with mine.
Johannes, the striver,
Shall through our active forces
Be raised on high to true existence.

The brothers in the temple
Held weighty council
How they might lead him from the depths
Aloft into the light-filled heights.
And they await from us
That we awake within his soul
The power to lofty flight.

You, my Philia, oh, breathe in
The light's clear sparkling essence
From sounding spaces,
And fill yourself with tones' delight
From out creative soul might,
That you can hand to me
The fair gifts which you gather
From spirit grounds.
For I can weave them then
Into the wakening sphere-bright-chiming.

And you, Astrid, O my spirit's
Beloved mirror-image,
Enquicken darkling power
In streaming light,
That colors thus may shine.
And organize all tonal being,
That weaving world-wide substance
Out-toning live.
For thus I can entrust
True spirit feeling to seeking human sense.

And you, O sturdy Luna,
As you are fortified within
Like to the living heart
That grows within the tree's deep core,

Unite now with your sisters' gifts
The image of your selfhood,
That certainty of knowledge
Be given the seeking soul.

PHILIA: I will enfill me
With clearest light-free-shine
From world-wide climes.
I will breathe heartward
Life-kindling strands of sound
From fields of ether,
That thus, beloved sister,
Your work may reach its goal.

ASTRID: I will enweave
Outstreaming light
With deepening darkness;
I will condense
The life of sound,
That glistening it may ring
And ringing it may glisten,
That you, beloved sister,
May guide the streaming rays of soul.

LUNA: I will enwarm the woof of soul
And will make hard life-giving ether.
They shall condense themselves,
They shall thus feel themselves,
And in themselves residing
Maintain creative force,
That you, beloved sister,
Within the seeking soul
May quicken certainty of knowledge.

MARIA: From Philia's wide climes
Shall stream forth joyfulness;
And undines' changing powers,
Let them now open
The soul's bright fluency —
That the awakened one
Experience
The world's delight,
The world's despair.
From Astrid's weaving
Shall spring forth love's own joy;
The sylphs' fair airy life,
Let it awaken
The soul's own sacrifice —
That the initiate
Revive and quicken
The sorrow-laden ones,
The joy beseechers.
From Luna's power
Shall stream forth firmness.
The fire beings' might,
It can create
The soul's own certainty —
That so the knowing one
Can find himself
In soul-enweaving,
In world-life-breathing.

PHILIA: I will now beg from world-wide spirits
That their true beings' light
Enchant the soul's own senses,
And that their words' clear clang
Delight the spirit's hearing —

           That he arise,
           The soon awakened one,
           On soul-world-ways
           To heaven's heights.

ASTRID: I will lead love's clear streams,
           The world all-warming ones,
           Unto the heart
           Of the neophyte —
           That he can thus bring down
           The heaven's kindness
           To earthly working,
           And consecration
           To human children.

LUNA: I will from primal rulers
           Beseech both power and courage,
           And lay them in the seeker
           Within his deep heart's core —
           That confidence
           In his own self
           Throughout his life
           May lead him on.
           He shall then feel himself
           Quite certain in himself.
           He shall from transient moments
           Then pluck the ripened fruits
           And call forth from them harvest
           For all eternity.

MARIA: With you, my sisters,
           United for noble work,
           I shall achieve
           What I so long for.

>	The cry of him
>	So sorely tested
>	Resounds in our light-filled world.

>	*(Johannes appears.)*

JOHANNES:
>	Oh, Maria, it is you!
>	My sorrow thus
>	Has born abundant fruit.
>	It's freed me from the phantom being
>	Which I had formed from out myself
>	And which then held me firmly fettered.
>	To pain I owe thus thanks
>	That on the path of soul
>	I could attain to you.

BENEDICTUS:
>	The weaving essence of the light streams forth
>	From man to man
>	To fill all the world with truth.
>
>	The grace of love pours forth its warmth
>	From soul to soul
>	To bring about the blessing of all worlds.
>
>	And spirit messengers, they wed
>	Man's consecrated work
>	With cosmic goals.
>
>	And when the man, who finds himself
>	In man, can wed one with the other,
>	Then spirit light streams forth through warmth
>	 of soul.

(From Scene X)

A Meditation Room

LUCIFER: O man, know thou me;
O man, feel thou thyself.
Thou hast freed thyself
From spirit guidance,
Hast taken refuge
In free earth realms.
Thou soughtst thine own true being
In earth confusion;
To find thyself
Was thy reward.
Use this reward.
Affirm thyself
In spirit daring.
Thou findst a foreign being
In wide, high realms.
It will confine thee
To human fate;
It will also oppress thee.
O man, feel thou thyself;
O man, know thou me.

AHRIMAN: O man, know thou thyself;
O man, feel thou me.
Thou hast escaped
From spirit darkness.
Thou hast attained
The light of earth.
So suck the power of truth
From my solidity.
I harden stable ground.

Thou canst, however, lose it.
In vacillation,
Thou scatterest the power of being.
And thou canst squander
In lofty light
The spirits' power.
Thou canst disintegrate.
O man, feel thou me;
O man, know thou thyself.

(They vanish.)

JOHANNES:
Oh, what is this; from out me — Lucifer
And after him then Ahriman!
Do I live through but new illusion
When ardently I cried for truth?
Thus Benedictus' brother summoned for me those
                      powers
Which activate illusion in men's souls.

(The following resounds as SPIRIT VOICE from the heights.)

SPIRIT VOICE:
Your thoughts are now descending
To world foundations.
What to soul illusion impelled you,
What in error has held you,
Appears to you in spirit light,
    Through whose fullness
    All men of vision
    In truth's light think;
    Through whose fullness
    All men of striving
    In loving live.

(From Scene XI)

THE SUN TEMPLE

(At the close of the scene Theodora appears.)

THEODORA:
>From out your heart
>There looms a sheen of light.
>A human image springs from it,
>And words can now be heard
>Which flow from this same human form.
>'Tis so they sound:
>>"I have now won myself
>>The power to reach the light."
>
>My friend, oh trust yourself!
>'Tis you, yourself, shall speak these words
>When once your time shall be fulfilled.

From
THE SOUL'S PROBATION

(From Scene I)

Capesius' study and library, in brown tones. Evening.

CAPESIUS: *(reading)*
    Within your thinking, cosmic thoughts have life.
    Within your feeling, cosmic forces weave.
    Within your willing, cosmic beings work.
    So lose yourself in cosmic thoughts,
    Experience yourself through cosmic forces,
    Create yourself out of will beings.
    End not in cosmic distances
    Through thinking's play of dream —
    Begin in spirit distances
    And end within your own soul depths.
    You'll find the goal of gods,
    Knowing in you yourself.

    (Three forms, as Soul Forces, hover about him.)

LUNA: The power fails you not
    For noble spirit flight.
    It is deep grounded
    In human willing.
    It is bright tempered
    By hope's high certainty.
    It is well steeled
    By clear far-future sight.
    The courage, only, fails you
    To pour into your willing
    Your full life-confidence.

                    Into the wide unknown
                    Make bold to dare your way.

ASTRID: From world-wide reaches
                    Out of sun-joyous-light —
                    From starry distances
                    Out of world-magic-might —
                    From blue bright heaven's ether
                    Out of high spirit power —
                    Aspire to might of soul
                    And lead its radiance
                    Into heart's ground;
                    Self-warming, then, will knowledge
                    Beget itself in thee.

THE OTHER PHILIA:
                    They would delude you,
                    The evil sisters;
                    They seek to weave you round
                    With life's phantasmal play.
                    It will dissolve —
                    This bright gift's idle fraud
                    Which they bestow on you
                    When you, with human power,
                    Would hold it fast.
                    They lead you out
                    To the world of gods
                    And will only destroy you,
                    If you, within their realm,
                    Would win by force
                    Your human being.

VOICE OF SPIRITUAL CONSCIENCE:
>Your thoughts are now descending
>To depths of human being.
>What as soul has enclosed you,
>What as spirit has been bound to you,
>Is released to world foundations;
>>From out whose fullness
>>All men, drinking,
>>In thinking live;
>>From out whose fullness
>>All men, living,
>>In semblance weave.

(From Scene II)

A Meditation Room, in violet tones.

MARIA:
>You, my sisters — whom I
>Can find in depths of being
>Each time my soul expands itself,
>And into cosmic distances
>Accompanies itself —
>Unbind for me the powers of sight
>From ether heights
>And lead them upon earthly paths,
>That in time's depths
>I may now ground myself
>And give myself direction
>Out of old ways of life
>Into new spheres of will.

PHILIA: I will now fill me
With striving soul-spun light
From heart's own deeps;
I will breathe inward
Life-kindling power of will
From spirit's urgings;
That you, beloved sister,
Within old spheres of life
May, finding, feel the light.

ASTRID: I will enweave
The feeling of selfhood's being
With love's surrendering will;
I will unbind
The quickening will-warm powers
From wishes fetters,
And will transform your laming longing
To finding-spirit-feeling;
That you, beloved sister,
On future earthly paths
May found and ground yourself.

LUNA: I will evoke renouncing powers of heart
And will make firm supporting peace of soul.
They shall wed one another
And strengthening-spirit-radiance
Raise upward from soul grounds;
They shall pervade each other
And harkening-spirit-hearing
Wrest from far earth realms,
That you, beloved sister,
Within time's wide existence
May find life-footprints there.

MARIA: *(after a pause)*
If I can but unloose myself
From bewildering self-feeling,
And may then give myself to you
So that my soul-life is reflected
By you from distant worlds,
I shall then free myself
From bonds of this life's orbit
And can then ground myself
In other ways of being.

(A longer pause, then the following):

MARIA: In you, my sisters, I see spirit beings
Who kindle souls out of the cosmic All.
The powers which quicken in eternity —
You can make ripe in man himself.
Through my soul's doorway I could often find
The path that wends into your realm,
And there behold with eyes of soul
The archetypal forms of earth existence.
I am now sorely needful of your help
For I'm obliged to find my way
From this my present pilgrimage in life
To long forgotten days of humankind.
Unbind for me my soul's existence from
                             self-feeling
Within its life in time.
Unlock for me the spheres of duty
Out of my by-gone paths of life.

VOICE OF SPIRITUAL CONSCIENCE:
    Her thoughts are now searching
    In the imprints in time.
    What as guilt still remains to her,
    What as duty is bidden her,
    Emerges from its soul foundations:
        From out whose depths
        All men, dreaming,
        Their lives are leading.
        Within whose depths
        All men, erring,
        Themselves are losing.

(From Scene III)

A friendly room, in rose-red tones.

(The Soul Forces speak to Johannes.)

LUNA: You cannot find yourself
    In mirror of another's soul.
    The force of your own being
    Must strike its roots deep into world foundations
    Would it transplant authentically
    The beauty from the spirit heights
    Into the depths of earth.
    Make bold to be yourself's own being
    That you, as strong soul form,
    Can sacrifice yourself to cosmic powers.

ASTRID: You should, upon your world-wide ways,
Not wish to lose yourself;
To sun-far-distances men do not reach
Who wish to rob themselves of their own being.
So make yourself now ready
To so press on through earthly love
In deep heart grounds
That World-All love may ripen.

THE OTHER PHILIA:
Oh, do not hear the sisters;
They lead you into world-wide wastes
And rob you of the earth's dear nearness.
They do not see how earthly love
Resembles cosmic love's own features.
Their beings reign within the cold,
Their forces flee away from warmth
And would entice all human beings
From their own soul depths
Into cold higher worlds.

(From Scene V)

A landscape, in which stands the Balde's lonely cottage.
   (Sitting on a bench, Dame Balde tells a fairy tale to Capesius.)

THE ROCK-SPRING-WONDER

DAME BALDE:
      There was one time a boy
      Who grew up as a poor wood-cutter's only child
      Within the forest's loneliness.
      Beside his loving parents
      He knew few other people.
      His body was of slender build,
      His skin — almost transparent,
      And one could look long in his eyes,
      They hid the deepest spirit-wonders.
      And though indeed few people
      Composed the circle of his life,
      He never was in want of friends.

      When in the nearby mountains
      Clear floods of golden sunlight glowed,
      The boy's deep pondering eye drew forth
      The spirit's gold into his soul
      Until his heart's whole being
      Grew like the morning sun. —
      But when through darkling clouds
      The morning sun-beams could not pierce,
      And dreariness had shrouded all the mountains,
      Then too his boyish eye grew dull,
      And sorrowful his heart ——.

So was he wholly one with all
The spirit weaving of his narrow world,
Which was thus no less strange to him
Than were his arms and limbs.
For friends to him were also all
The forest trees and flowers;
Bright spirit beings spoke from their coronas,
From calix and from tree-top,
And he could understand their whisperings. —
So hidden world-wide wonder-things
Were unsealed to the boy
When oft his soul held converse
With what for many people
Appeared to be but lifeless.

Yet, of an evening, oft, with deep concern,
His parents missed their treasured offspring.
He was then at a spot close by
Where from the virgin rock a spring broke forth,
And, bursting into thousand particles,
The water drops fell splashing on the stones.
And when the moonlight's silver glance
In sparkling rainbow-play, all magically,
Was mirrored in the tide of falling drops,
Then could the boy for hours on end
Sit rooted by the spring.
And figures, builded spirit-wise,
Emerged before his boyish seer-gaze
In rushing water and in moonlight's glinting
                              glimmer,
Till they became three women's forms,
Who spoke to him about those things
Toward which the current of his soul was urging.

So when upon a mild mid-summer night,
The boy was sitting by the stream once more,
One of these women caught up many thousand
                              particles
Of those pied water drops' pure being
And handed them unto the second woman.
She formed from out the thousand star-drops
A silver gleaming chalice-vessel,
And handed it in turn unto the third.
She filled it with the moon's pure silver light
And gave it thus the boy,
Who had beheld all this the while
With his same boyish seer-vision.

But in the night which followed
On this event he dreamed
A wild and dreadful dragon
Had robbed him of the pure bright vessel. —

After this night the boy experienced
But three times more the rock-spring wonder;
And then the women came no more,
Although the boy sat pondering
Beside the rock-born spring in silver moonlight.

And when three hundred sixty weeks
Had run their course for the third time,
The boy had long become a man;
Had journeyed from his parents' home and forest
                              valley
To settle in a far strange city.
And there one evening, tired
From all his hard day's labor,
He pondered long what life held still in store
                              for him —

When suddenly he felt himself
Transported to his rock-born spring,
And could behold the water-women once again,
And this time — hear them speak.

The first one said to him:
Oh, think on me in every moment,
When you feel lonely on life's path.
I lure the gaze of human souls
To ether reaches and to star-wide heights.
And he who will but feel me,
To him I offer the life-draught of hope
From out my wonder-goblet. —

And then the second spoke:
Forget me not in those grave moments
Which threaten your life's font of courage.
I lead the urge of human hearts
To soul foundations and to spirit heights.
And he who seeks his strength from me,
For him I smithy the life-steel of faith
With my bright wonder-hammer. —

The third one could be heard as follows:
To me lift up your spirit-eye
When deep life-riddles storm upon you.
I spin the gleaming threads of thought
In long life-labyrinths, and in depths of soul.
And he who harbors trust in me,
For him I work the warm life-rays of love
Upon my wonder-weaving-loom. —

And in the night which followed
On this experience
The man dreamed that a dreadful dragon
Was prowling in great circles round him,
But could not now come near him:
He was protected from the fearsome beast
By these same beings, whom he had once beheld
                              beside the spring.
And who had traveled with him
From his fair homeland to this distant place.

―――

Much later in this scene, when Johannes encounters his Doubleganger, the Voice of Conscience *is once again heard, followed by the appearance of Lucifer and Ahriman.*

THE VOICE OF CONSCIENCE:
        So speaks concealed,
        Still unrepealed,
        Not yet revealed,
        In blood still sealed,
        Deep hidden power
        Of passion's dower.

―――

Lucifer and Ahriman appear.

LUCIFER:
O man, subdue thyself;
O man, deliver me.
Thou hast overcome me
Within thy soul's high realms;
I stay still intergrown with thee,
Within thy being's deeps.
Thou shalt thus always find me
Upon thy lone life-trails
Shouldst thou attempt to shield thee
Entirely from me.
O man, subdue thyself;
O man, deliver me.

AHRIMAN:
O man, embolden thee;
O man, experience me.
Thou canst now employ in thee
The spirit's sight;
I had to destroy for thee
Thy heart's quick life;
Thou shalt oft have to suffer
The keenest soul tortures
If humbly thou dost not
Adhere unto my forces.
O man, embolden thee;
O man, experience me.

———

(From Scene IX)

A Woodland Pasture in the Middle Ages.

(Dame Balde — at that time Dame Keena — tells a fairy tale.)

DAME KEENA:
    There was one time a man
    Who pondered much about the world and things.
    It was the greatest torture for his brain
    To try to understand the source of evil.
    Here he could simply give himself no answer.
    "The whole world comes from God," he told himself,
    "And God can only have the good within him.
    How do bad people spring out of the good?"
    Thus constantly he pondered quite in vain;
    The answer simply was not to be found.
    Whereon it chanced one day that this poor ponderer
    Beheld before him on his path a tree
    Which was in conversation with an axe;
    And lo, this axe was saying to the tree:
    "What's quite impossible for you, this I can do.
    For I can fell you; but you not me."
    Whereon the tree responded to the haughty axe:
    "A year ago a man obtained the wood
    From which he formed and finished off your handle
    Out of my body with another axe."
    And when the man had heard this conversation,
    There rose unsought within his soul a thought
    Which he could not put clearly into words,
    But which gave him full answer to the question:
    How evil can arise out of the good.

(From Scene X)

The landscape in which stands the Balde's lonely cottage.

> *(Capesius awakens out of the vision which has revealed to his soul his former incarnation in the Middle Ages.)*

A VOICE AS SPIRIT CONSCIENCE: *(at the close of the scene)*
    Refeel, what you have seen;
    Relive, what you have done.
    You are now newly sprung to being.
    You have but dreamed your life.
    Enact it now
        Through noble spirit light;
        Perceive your earth-world tasks
        With power of soul sight.
        If this you cannot do,
        You're caught in empty naught
        Throughout eternity.

(From Scene XIII)

THE SUN TEMPLE

PHILIA: I will enfill me
               With faith's clear power of light;
               I will breathe heartward
               The living strength of trust
               From soul-glad eager striving,
               That the spirit-sleeper
               Be wakened by the light.

ASTRID: I will enweave
              Exhalted revelation's word
             With humble joy of soul;
             I will condense
             The rays of hope.
             It shall in darkness shine,
             It shall in light glow duskward,
             That the spirit-sleeper
             Be carried by strong forces.

LUNA: I will enwarm the light of soul
            And will make firm the power of love.
            They shall thus embolden themselves,
            They shall thus redeem themselves
            And raising themselves aloft,
            Will to give themselves weight,
            That the spirit-sleeper
            Be released from all world-burdens,
            And so can be set free
            By soul-light-joy.

From
THE GUARDIAN OF THE THRESHOLD

(From Scene II)

A Room, indigo-blue in tone.

(At the close of the scene, Maria and Johannes Thomasius remain in the room after the other characters leave. The three spirit-forms, Philia, Astrid, and Luna, appear in a cloud of light. The following is the spiritual experience of Johannes Thomasius.)

PHILIA: The soul is athirst
To drink of the light,
That wells forth from worlds,
Which nurturing will
Cloaks over for man.
Grown ardent to harken
The spirit is tempted
By the converse of gods,
Which the goodness of wisdom
Holds hid from the heart.
Endangerment threatens
The thoughts that are delving
In realms of the soul,
Where far from the senses
What is hidden holds sway.

ASTRID: Souls widen themselves,
Who follow the light
And penetrate worlds,
Which courageful seeing
Lays open to man.
To live in full blessing
The spirit is questing
In realms of the gods,
Which radiant wisdom
Proclaims to the seer.
What is deep hidden beckons
The dauntless desiring
For open world-reaches,
Which far from all thinking
Hold treasured deep secrets.

LUNA: The soul bears ripe fruit
To build its own seeing
That's sprung of those forces,
Which fearless free willing
Enkindles in man.
From primal foundations
Delivering forces
Draw forth magic powers
Still hid from the senses
Through earth limitations.
And souls who are seeking
Are following footprints
In search of the portal
The gods have closed firmly
To man's erring willing.

THE VOICE OF CONSCIENCE:
    Your thoughts are now in quandry
    At the chasm of being.
    What was lent you as support,
    You have now lost it.
    What has lit your way as sun,
    Has now gone out.
    You err now in the depths of worlds,
    Which mankind, drunk with longing,
    Would seek to conquer.
    You tremble in the grounds of growth,
    Where mankind must forego
    Soul consolation.

MARIA: Incline your soul now nigh
    To love's own powers,
    Which once could permeate all hope for you
    With warmth of life,
    Which once could light up all your will for you
    With spirit light.
    Wrest free from loneliness
    The seeking strong heart-forces,
    And feel your friend's close nearness
    In darknesses of striving.

THOMASIUS:
    Where was I in this moment? My soul-forces
    Uncovered the confusion deep within me;
    And cosmic conscience then revealed to me
    What I have lost; in blessing sounded then
    The voice of love within the realms of darkness.

———

(From Scene VI)

A space which is not confined by walls, but closed in by intertwining tree-like plants and forms. The whole is in violent motion and at times filled with storm.

BENEDICTUS:
>Win yourself in cosmic power of thought,
>And lose yourself through life of cosmic forces;
>You find earth-destinations, mirroring
>Themselves through your own being, in world-light.

VOICES, which sound together, spoken by
PHILIA, ASTRID, LUNA:
>Now thoughts hover near
>Like weaving of dreams
>Arising as beings
>Essential to souls;
>Self-quickening will,
>Self-wakening feeling,
>Self-fashioning thinking
>Emerge for the dreamer.

LUCIFER: Within your willing cosmic beings work.

AHRIMAN: The cosmic beings, they bewilder you.

LUCIFER: Within your feeling cosmic forces weave.

AHRIMAN: The cosmic forces, they inveigle you.

LUCIFER: Within your thinking cosmic thoughts have life.

AHRIMAN: The cosmic thoughts, they are perplexing you.

VOICES OF PHILIA, ASTRID, LUNA:
>Now thoughts hovered near
>Like weaving of dreams
>Arising as beings
>Essential to souls;
>Self-quickening will,
>Self-wakening feeling,
>Self-fashioning thinking
>Emerged for the dreamer.

(Later in the scene Dame Balde appears and tells a fairy tale.)

DAME BALDE:
>There was upon a time a god-bright child
>Akin to beings privileged to guide
>And weave the wisdom of the spirit realms.
>Brought up with care by Truth's almighty Father,
>It grew, within his world, to primal power;
>And when it felt the swift creative stir
>Of ripened will within its limbs of light,
>It often looked with pity toward the earth
>Where human souls long ever after truth.
>The child then said to mighty Father Truth:
>"Men thirst, O Father, for the drink
>Which you can offer them from out your springs."
>Then earnestly great Father Truth replied:
>"The springs which I must ever tend and guard,
>They let the light stream forth from spirit suns;
>And only those are free to drink the light
>Who need not ever thirst for air to breathe.

On light, therefore, I have reared up the child
Who feels compassion for the souls on earth
And can engender light in breathing beings.
So go, my child, and wend your way to men
And lead the light within them, spirit kindled,
Confidently forth to meet my light."

Thereon the bright Light-Being made its way
Unto those souls who live their lives in breathing.
It found on earth full many goodly mortals
Who offered it soul-lodging joyously.
In faithful love it led their soul-gaze thence
Unto the Father at the Springs of Light.
And when this Being heard from human lips
And happy human musing, *phantasy*,
That magic word, with joy it felt itself
Alive and warm in goodly human hearts.

One day, however, there approached this Being
A man, who cast upon it hostile looks.
"I lead the souls of men upon the earth
To Father Truth who tends the Springs of Light."
Thus spoke this Being to the unknown man.
Whereon the man replied: "You weave wild dreams
In human spirits and deceive their souls."
And since that day which saw this come to pass,
Full many men heap slander on this Being
Who can bring Light to breathing human souls.

(Philia, Astrid, Luna and the Other Philia appear.)

PHILIA:
The soul shall discover,
That drinks of the light,
In world-wide expanses
'Tis keenly awake.

ASTRID:
The spirit shall feel,
That knows itself fearless,
When one with the world
'Tis strongly arisen.

LUNA:
The man on earth wills,
Who strives toward the heights,
In depths of all being
To be mightily rooted.

THE OTHER PHILIA:
The man on earth strives
Toward the bearers of light,
Who unlock the worlds
That liven and quicken
Glad senses in men.
Bespirited wonder
Bears upward the spirit
To god-bright expanses,
That waken in soul-depths
Their radiant beauty.
Achievement gives comfort
To feelings that dare
To tread upon thresholds,
Which sternly are guarded
From souls full of fear.

And staunchness discovers
The ripening will,
Which bears itself fearless
To powers creative
Sustaining the worlds.

(From Scene VII)

A landscape of imaginative forms, majestic in its combination of surging masses of water — which form themselves into pictures — and flaming eddies of fire.

THE OTHER PHILIA: *(at the close of the scene)*
Oh, do not heed the strict, stern Guardian.
He leads you into barren life
And robs you of all warmth of soul;
He can see only spirit being
And knows not human anguish
Which souls can only bear
If earthly love protects them
From far, cold cosmic reaches.
Strict sternness lives in him,
Mild gentleness flees far from him;
And wish-full forces —
'Tis these he hates
Since earth's age-old beginning.

(From Scene IX)

A friendly, sunny landscape. Morning. In the background a large city with many factories.

MARIA: Johannes, your soul has won now for itself
True knowledge out of icy realms of truth.
And you will now no longer weave in pictures
What souls, only in bodies, live as dream.
For far from world-becoming are those thoughts
Which would beget themselves out of themselves.

THOMASIUS:
And that they do so, springs out of self-love,
Which seeks to show itself as thirst for knowledge.

MARIA: He who would actively serve human progress
And would accomplish works, which with real being
Can act as forces in the course of time,
Must first entrust himself to powers, which,
                  battling
In deep realities, bring into order,
Or into chaos, measure as well as number.
For knowledge, in deepest truth, is only life
Which can become revealed in human souls
When they can recollect in earthly bodies
Experiences from the spirit realms.

———

MARIA: *(at the close of the scene)*
Whether you walk in error or in truth,
You can always maintain an open view
To let your soul pursue its further course
If you bear bravely the necessities
Which stem out of the life of spirit realms.

(From Scene X)

The Temple of a Mystic Brotherhood.

MARIA: When he, the great Light Bringer, rays forth wisdom,
And fills the world with prideful sense of self,
That brightly lights the selfhood of all beings
Through his bold nature as an archetype,
Then led by him, man's inmost soul may bring
Into appearance — with fresh joy of sense,
And raying wisdom's gladness all about it —
What lives itself and loves itself through life.
But human beings are, above all other spirits,
In deep need of that God Who does not only
Demand amaze when He reveals Himself
In beauty to the soul in outer life,
But first rays forth His highest power then
When dwelling in the soul's own innermost,
And lovingly, in death, announces life.
So man may turn to Lucifer to feel
With full enthusiasm light and beauty,
And through him thus experience himself —
But should, as his own being, never *will* him.

Yet to the other Spirit man calls out
When he can rightly understand himself:
It is on earth the soul's true goal of love:
Not I, the Christus lives within my being.

(The Four Soul Forces appear at the close of the scene.)

THE OTHER PHILIA:
Now thoughts are ascending
From mystery places in offering
To primal foundations;
What in souls has life,
What in spirits has light,
Is freed now from the world of forms; —
And cosmic presences stoop down
In grace to human beings,
Through soul powers
The spirit's light
To kindle.

PHILIA:
I will now beg from world-wide spirits
That their bright beings' light
Uphold the soul's own senses,
And that their words' clear clang
Unbind the spirit's hearing,
That what has been awakened
On soul-world-ways
Be not extinguished
In human life.

ASTRID: I will lead love's clear streams,
The world all-warming ones,
Unto the spirit
Of the neophyte,
That breath of consecration
In human hearts
Maintain itself.

LUNA: I will, from primal rulers,
Beseech both power and courage,
And make them the strong helpers
Of sacrificial will,
That it may thus transform
What time beholds
To spirit harvest
For all eternity.

PROSE PASSAGES

Concerning
and including

THE DREAM SONG
of
OLAF ÅSTESON

This ancient Norwegian folk song first came to light about 1850. It was discovered in a lonely valley in Telemark, Norway, by a clergyman named Landstad. No one seems to know how long it had been handed down by word of mouth, but it is certainly very old.

It was brought to Rudolf Steiner's attention, and he discussed it at some length with the Norwegian writer, Ingeborg Möller. She helped him with regard to the unusual forms of the early language in which the song still lives, and from it he made a German rendering. Thereafter he spoke in many lectures of its deep meaning and spiritual significance, particularly on three occasions when it was recited in the German by Marie Steiner at New Year's time in 1912, 1913 and 1914. He also made eurythmy forms for it, and since then it has frequently been recited and performed in eurythmy at the Goetheanum.

The following English translation is from Rudolf Steiner's German rendering, and the passages preceding and following it are from his lecture on New Year's Eve, 1914.

*

We will begin our celebration for the year's end with the recitation of the beautiful Norwegian legend of Olaf Åsteson:* Olaf Åsteson, who, as the time of Christmas approached, fell into a sort of sleep that lasted for thirteen days, the thirteen holy days and nights. . . .

On former occasions, we have seen how through spiritual science it is possible to win again for the human cognition of today, ancient treasures of knowledge. This knowledge of an earlier time rested upon the fact that, as man was constituted at that time, it was possible for him, under certain circumstances, to dip down as human microcosm into the laws and happenings of the macrocosm, and so to have soul experiences that were of an intimately stirring nature. . . .

*In Åsteson, Å is pronounced ŏ as in lŏst. In Brooksvalin, p. 170, lin is pronounced lēn, ē as in ēve.

Olaf Åsteson, Olaf the Son of the Earth, experienced, during the thirteen shortest days of the year, while he was thus dipped into the macrocosm, manifold secrets of the world-all, involving also the penetration of Christianity into the North....

So let us hear these experiences.

THE DREAM SONG OF OLAF ÅSTESON

From the Ancient Norwegian

I

So listen to my song,
For I will sing you
About a sturdy stripling!
    It was young Olaf Åsteson,
    Who once did sleep so long,
    Of him I will now sing you.

II

He went to rest on Christmas Even.
A mighty sleep o'ercame him soon,
And nowise could he waken
Till on the thirteenth day
The folk were gone to church.
    It was young Olaf Åsteson,
    Who once did sleep so long,
    Of him I will now sing you.

He went to rest on Christmas Even,
And long had he slept — ah long!
For no way could he waken
Till on the thirteenth day
The snow-bird spread out her wings.
          It was young Olaf* ......

No way could Olaf waken
Till on the thirteenth day
The sun gleamed over the mountain.
Then saddled he his eager steed
And rode to church with greatest speed.
          It was young Olaf ....

There stood the priest
At altar reading the mass
When Olaf stepped in the doorway
And set him down to tell
Of many wondrous dream-lands
That in his long, long sleeping
Spread far before his soul.
          It was young Olaf ....

And young as well as aged people
They listened awestruck to the words
That Olaf spoke about his dreams.
          It was young Olaf Åsteson,
          Who once did sleep so long,
          Of him I will now sing you.

---

*The refrains are repeated throughout.

III

I went to rest on Christmas Even.
A mighty sleep o'ercame me soon.
And nowise could I waken
Till on the thirteenth day
The folk were gone to church.
        The moon shone bright
        And far off led the lonely ways.

I was borne aloft to cloudy heights
And hurled to the bottom of the sea
And who would follow me —
No happiness can be his lot.
        The moon shone bright
        And far off led the lonely ways.

I was borne aloft to cloudy heights
And thrust again in brackish mire —
Beholding all hell's terrors
As well as heaven's light.
        The moon shone . . . .

I had to pass through earth-dark-deeps
Where the gods' great torrents rage and roar.
To look on them was not granted me
But well I could hear their rushing.
        The moon shone . . . .

My ebon steed neighed now no more,
My hounds no longer bayed,
Nor did the dawn-bird sing her song.
There was a single wonder over all.
        The moon shone . . . .

I had to traverse, in spirit-lands,
The thorny moorland's endless waste.
All ripped and torn was my scarlet mantle
And broken the nails of my feet.
          The moon shone ....

I came to the Bridge of Gjallar.
In highest windy height it hangs.
'Tis welded all of fine red gold
And countless pointed nails it has.
          The moon shone ....

I was lashed and stung by the spirit-snake
And bitten by the spirit-hound;
The steer, stood middle in the way.
They are the bridge's three dread creatures;
Of fearful evil power are they!
          The moon shone ....

The hound has a savage bite,
The snake a searing sting.
The steer — his thrust is mighty.
And they let no one over the bridge
Who will not honour truth.
          The moon shone ....

I passed over the Gjallar Bridge.
'Tis narrow and dizzily high.
Through swamps I had to wade —
They lie now behind me!
          The moon shone ....

Through swamps I had to wade
That bottomless were to my feet.
And as I stepped across the bridge,
The grit of earth was in my mouth
As 'tis with those beneath the sod.
    The moon shone ....

I came to waters, then
Wherein, like clear blue flames,
The pale ice-masses glistened bright.
And God, he led my sense
That I might shun that place.
    The moon shone ....

To Winter's path I turned my steps.
Upon the right it lay. —
I looked as if into Paradise
That far off streamed and sparkled.
    The moon shone ....

And God's high holy Mother,
I saw her there in beauty.
To travel now toward Brooksvalin
She bade me, making known
That souls encounter judgment there.
    The moon shone bright
     And far off led the lonely ways.

———

IV

In other worlds I whiled me now
Through many a dark night long.
And God alone can know
How much distress of soul I saw.
      In Brooksvalin, where mortals
      Must undergo the Judgment Day.

I could behold a youthful man,
Had murdered once a little boy.
And now he had to bear him
Forever on his arm!
He stood in slime so deep.
      In Brooksvalin, where mortals
      Must undergo the Judgment Day.

An aged man I saw, too.
He wore a great cloak of lead.
For thus was he punished, that he
Had lived in greed on earth.
      In Brooksvalin . . . .

And men appeared before me
Clad all in clothes of flame.
Dishonesty weighed grimly
Upon their meager souls.
      In Brooksvalin . . . .

And children I could see
With glowing coals beneath their feet.
They wronged their parents on the earth.
This hurt their spirits sorely.
    In Brooksvalin . . . .

And I must needs draw near
A strange and awful house
Where witches had to labour
In blood they tortured on the earth.
    In Brooksvalin . . . .

From northward came in great wild hordes
A-riding evil spirits
Led on by Hell's dark chieftain.
    In Brooksvalin . . . .

What from the northward came
Was more than all else evil.
Ahead rode he, the hell-dark chief
Upon his steel-black stallion.
    In Brooksvalin . . . .

But from the southward came
In noble quiet other hosts.
A-fore rode on Saint Michael
At Jesu Christi's side.
    In Brooksvalin . . . .

The souls that were sin beladen
They trembled with awesome fear.
Their tears flowed down in rivers
That sprang from evil doing.
          In Brooksvalin . . . .

In majesty stood Michael
And weighed the human souls
Upon his flashing scales.
And judging stood beside him
The World-Judge, Jesus Christ.
          In Brooksvalin, where mortals
          Must undergo the Judgment Day.

V

How bless'd is he who in earthly life
Gives shoes unto the poor!
He need not then with naked feet
A-wander in thorny fields.
          So speaks the tongue of the scales
          And truth almighty
          Rings out through Spirit-Worlds.

How bless'd is he who in earthly life
Hands bread unto the poor!
For then they cannot harm him,
The hounds in yonder world.
          So speaks the tongue . . . .

How bless'd is he who in earthly life
Brings grain unto the poor!
For then the steer's sharp horn
Can threaten him no more
When he must cross the Gjallar Bridge.
        So speaks the tongue ....

How bless'd is he who in earthly life
Gives clothes unto the poor!
He cannot then be frozen
By ice in Brooksvalin.
        So speaks the tongue of the scales
        And truth almighty
        Rings out through Spirit-Worlds.

VI

And young as well as aged people
They listened awestruck to the words
That Olaf spoke about his dreams.
        You've slept so long — ah long!
        Awaken now, O Olaf Åsteson!

We have heard in this legend the message of an ancient knowledge, an ancient insight into the spiritual world, which must be won anew through a spiritual-scientific world conception. Often we hear the statement, which is found in all communications concerning the entrance of the human soul into the spiritual world, that man can only then perceive this spiritual world when he comes to the gate of death and then plunges into the elements....

All this is described here in a wonderfully stirring way, and is brought together with the manner in which the human soul lives within the secrets of the spiritual world. But much in this legend, as it is today, is no longer as it originally was. Originally, without doubt, there was a still more vivid description, first of the experiences of the earth-realm, then the water-realm; and then the air and fire realms were more differentiated than these aftertones which have come down into the present; the whole made a far mightier, far more majestic impression in the tremendous grandeur of the original language, the superhumanly moving element that lay in such folk legends.

In such times as the present, there is much need to ponder the fact that humanity, although with a more dim, twilight consciousness, was of old permeated by a knowledge that has been lost and must be regained.... We can indeed say that while one part of the human soul has been founding our materialistic culture, the other part, which was of old more wakeful, has slept.... During this time, with regard to spiritual knowledge, humanity has truly been: Olaf Åsteson. It has truly! Only that this humanity has not yet awakened! Spiritual science must awaken it. The time must come when "young as well as aged people" hear the words that will be spoken out of that part of the human soul which has slept during the dark age.

Long has the human soul slept, but spiritual beings will come to it and will call to it: "Awaken now, O Olaf Åsteson!"

We must prepare ourselves now rightly so that we will not be met by this call: "Awaken now, O Olaf Åsteson!" and not have ears to hear it....

On this New Year night, let us bring the microcosm of our experience into connection with the macrocosm of the experience of humanity encompassing the entire earth; then we will be able to experience a fore-sense of the dawn of the great new World-Day, at the first breaking light of which we stand, seeking to experience worthily its midnight.

Concerning

BEAUTY, TRUTH, GOODNESS

LOVE AND FREEDOM

These quotations from various lectures and books by Rudolf Steiner, as they are translated here, have, in many cases, been cut or condensed according to the needs of the special occasions when they were used.

They are arranged in a sequence according to the themes, thus adding a further aspect to the scope of this volume, as mentioned in the Foreword.

The sources from which they are taken are listed at the back.

> The shadow cast by the Spirit in space
> Is beauty.
> This shadow becomes a living being
> Through the artist's creative spirit.[1]

However long people may ponder how to banish from the world, through outer means, crime and wrong — true healing of evil into good will lie for the human soul, in future, in the fact that *true art* will pour like a spiritual fluid into human souls and human hearts; so that these souls and hearts of men when they are wisely surrounded by what has been created as architectural, sculptural and other art forms, will — if they are given to lying — cease to lie, or — if they are given to breaking the peace — will cease to disturb the peace of their fellow men. Buildings, for instance, will begin to speak. They will speak a language of which today people do not even dream.

Just as the spirits of nature have given to man a larynx, similarly we put at the disposal of the universe such an organ when we create the right artistic forms. They become then the means whereby the gods can speak to us.... *Art is the creation of organs through which the gods can speak to man.*[2]

It is out of the soil of *ugliness* that man's enthusiasm for the beautiful springs forth. This is a cosmic secret, my dear friends. We need the sharp goad of all that is ugly in order that beauty may come to light.

And the greatest artistic natures have been those who through their bodily constitution have been strong enough to bear being infested by these spiders of the elemental world, in order to bring forth a Sistine Madonna, or the like. — What is created in the world as beauty is brought forth entirely in such a way that it arises out of a sea of ugliness through the *enthusiasm* of the human soul.[3]

Only what is *chaotic* can be made beautiful. When we transform the chaos in the cosmos, beauty arises. *Chaos* and *cosmos* are thus interchangeable concepts. The cosmos — which means the beautiful world — cannot be created out of earthly things, but only out of chaos. And what we make out of earthly things is only an imitation, within matter, of already formed chaos.

> To have a sense for beauty means
> for man, not to deny in the physical world
> his connection with the spirit.[4]

We may easily ask why the gods, or God, has created *suffering*. Suffering must be there if the world is to arise in its beauty.

Upon the soil of suffering *all beauty* rests. Beauty can only develop out of pain. This pain, this suffering — we must be able to feel, to experience it. Only by undergoing suffering are we able to truly find our way into the supersensible worlds.

And this may already be said of experiences at another level. Everyone who has gained even a little knowledge will be able to admit and will say to you: For what I have experienced in life as joy and good fortune, I am thankful to my destiny. *Knowledge*, however, I have won only through my suffering, through my pain.[5]

If we were to speak more deeply of painting, the significance of the connection between the inner soul-life of the universe and *colour* would reveal itself. It would be meaningless ever to paint with colours, if colours were not something very different from what they appear to be to outer physical perception....

Colour is the language of nature's soul, the speech of the soul of the universe.[6]

As we may say of *truth* that it makes us *free* — when we grasp it ideally and also in a spiritual-scientific manner — so we must say that in *beauty* we find again our *connection with the world*. And man cannot exist without living freely within himself, and without finding his connection with the world about him. Man finds his individuality in free thought, and he finds the possibility of himself bringing what the world has made of him into connection again with the world itself, by ascending into the realm of *beauty*, into the realm of *art*.[7]

In ancient Greece, it was said that all human striving after knowledge must proceed from *wonder*. Let us grasp this in the positive sense that in every soul who seeks to reach to the *truth* there must at one time be present this experience of standing in awe before the universe.

When, irrespective of all other circumstances, a human being sets out from an experience of wonder over the phenomena of the world, then this has the same result as if we were to put a seed into the earth out of which a plant will grow. For all knowledge must, in a certain respect, have as its seed-kernel — wonder.

Someone may be the most astute thinker, but if he has never passed through this stage of wonderment, nothing will come of it; it will be a keen-sighted, clever linking of ideas, comprising nothing which is not correct — but what is correct does not necessarily reach reality. What is essential is that before we begin to think, before we set our thinking in motion, we shall have gone through this condition of wondering. Thought which sets itself in motion without this will remain merely a spinning of ideas. For thinking must "originate," if we may use this term, in wonder....

Yet this is still not sufficient if we are to attain to the reality of truth....

Wonder, *veneration*, being in wise *harmony* with world phenomena, *surrender* to the course of cosmic events, these are the progressive stages of development which we must undergo and which must always run parallel with thought — which must never desert our thinking — otherwise our thinking will attain merely to what is correct, what is right in the ordinary sense, but never to the truth in its reality.[8]

The universe seen from within is light; seen from without, by spiritual perception, it is thought. The human head seen from within is thought, seen from without — light.

As human beings we have light within us. Only it does not appear to us as light, because we live in it, because, as we use it, it becomes in us — thought. We are light beings, but do not know it.

This is one of the world secrets. We look out into the universe. It is flooded with light. In the light lives thought. But in this thought-permeated light lives a dying world. In light the world of the past is continually dying, and as it dies, it shines in beauty.

Thought perceived spiritually appears as *light*.

If, on the other hand, we look at *will* spiritually, it becomes always thicker and thicker until it becomes *matter*.... And in this matter — that is, in will — is revealed finally the continually beginning, constantly germinating world.... For the world of the future arises in darkness, in the element of material will. It lies hidden in the strength of matter, while the past is what shines in the beauty of light.

And just as the world about us may be regarded in this way as a working together of darkness and light, so our own inner selves, in so far as they expand within space, can also be seen as light and darkness. Only that for our own consciousness, light is thought, imagination; while the darkness is, in us, will, which becomes at length goodness, becomes love. In this interaction we constantly permeate our thoughts with the will from the rest of our organism. And precisely what we call purest thought is light, the remains of our ancient past, permeated by will. Here is the germinal point of freedom. Pure thought is permeated by will — the seed of what is to be — which will unfold into the far distant future and, in turn, in dying, give forth light.[9]

In the light, live dying world-thoughts; in the forces of weight live worlds to be, through the seeds of will. All this streams through the souls moving in space.

When we realize this, we look at the world both physically and morally at the same time. The physical and moral do not appear side by side. No, they are only different aspects of what in itself is one entity.

The meaningful, moral world-order reveals itself out of the natural world-order.[9]

We see about us today a world of light; millions of years ago it was a *moral world*. We bear within us a moral world, which, millions of years hence, will be a world of light.... And a great feeling of responsibility toward the world-to-be wells up in us, because our moral impulses will later become shining worlds....

Here, in this great course of cosmic development, we can speak of *goodness* only when there is a clear distinction between inner and outer world, so that the good is *free* to follow the impulses of the spiritual world, or not to follow them. It is only in this way, through the free deed, that true goodness can come into being.

As the world of sleep — in which we are united spiritually with the inner nature of what surrounds us — has to do with truth, and the dreaming state with beauty, so the condition of wakefulness, when freedom is possible, has to do with goodness, with the good.... And here the impulse to arouse ourselves, to *awaken* — touches the very nerve of our present time.[9]

From deeds of *love*, we have nothing to benefit our own egotism, yet the world has all the more from them. Spiritual research tells us that love is for the whole world what the sun is for external life. No soul could any longer grow and flourish anywhere were love taken from the world. Love is the moral sun of the universe.

———

With the gradual development of selfishness, evil came into the world. Yet this had to happen because the good could not be grasped without the evil. Through man's victory over himself, the possibility is given for the unfolding of love. Christ brought to man, who was sinking ever deeper into egotism, the impulse for this overcoming of himself, and thereby the power to conquer evil. The deed of Christ on Golgotha, for the entire world, brings together once more all those who were separated by self-seeking. True in the deepest sense are thus Christ's words when He says: *Inasmuch as ye have done it unto one of the least of these my bretheren, ye have done it unto me.*

This deed of love of the Godhead has flooded back over the earthly world; little by little it will stream throughout the entire development of humanity and, in spite of the forces of physical decay, will imbue man with new spiritual life — because it was done not out of egotism, but purely out of the spirit of love.

———

Wisdom that is permeated with love, which not only furthers the world, but leads it to the Christ Being — such love-filled wisdom also *excludes all lie*. For a lie is the direct opposite of fact; and whosoever gives himself over lovingly to the facts does not lie. The lie springs from egotism — without exception. When, through love, we have found the way to wisdom, then we shall actually have penetrated to this wisdom through an ever increasing power of self-conquest — through selfless love. And thereby man becomes a free personality.

Evil was the dark ground, the sub-soil, into which the light of love could shine. And it is this light of love which enables us to recognize the meaning of evil, the place of evil in the world. For just as the light itself would not be apprehended without the darkness, so love is only enhanced through the overcoming of evil. Only the free human being, in this sense, becomes a true Christian.[10]

It is Christ's intention that the realm, of which He has said: "*My kingdom is not of this world,*" shall in very truth enter into those parts of the human being which are themselves not of this world — which are of another world. For in each of us there lies that part of man which is "not of this world." And this part must seek intensively for that Kingdom of which Christ has said it is "not of this world."

We live today in a time when this must be understood. Many such things in human development announce themselves through deep contrast. And in our time, too, such a mighty, significant happening announces itself through contrast. For the time will come, with the coming Christ, the ever-present Christ, when men will learn to ask advice, not only for their own souls, but for what they want to accomplish, to found, here on earth through their eternal natures — to ask, to put questions to the Christ Being.

Christ is not a ruler of men, He is a brother of men Who wants to be asked in every detail of life.... The time must come, it must not be long in coming, when the eternal part of the human soul will put the question to the Christ regarding what it intends to do: Shall it be done, or shall it not be done? — when the human soul will see beside him the Christ as loving companion in all circumstances of life and receive from Him, not only comfort, not only strength, but also receive advice concerning what should happen.

The Kingdom of Christ Jesus is *not* of this world, but it must work *in* this world, and human souls must become the instruments of the Kingdom that is not of this world.

Humanity must learn to ask, to put questions to the Christ Being.

How can this be done? This can only be done through learning His language.... And the fact that we learn through spiritual science to speak inwardly with the spiritual world, this is far more important than that we acquire theoretical thoughts. *For the Christ is with us always unto the ends of the earth.* And we should learn His language. Through what we hear of the manifold secrets of world development, the so-called teachings and laws of spiritual science, we acquire a language into which we can pour questions that we can put to the spiritual world. And when we learn rightly how to speak inwardly in the language of this spiritual life, then it will come about that the Christ will appear at our side and will answer us.

This is something which we should hold as an attitude of heart, as a feeling, in our striving for a science of the spirit.

For why do we occupy ourselves with spiritual science? It is as though we should learn, in doing so, the vocabulary of this language through which we can approach the Christ. And he who makes the effort to learn to think about the world, as is striven for by spiritual science, who exerts his mind in this manner, in order to penetrate into the secrets of the world, to him — out of the dark grounds of these world secrets — the Christ Jesus will come, and will be the brotherly, guiding power in which he lives, so that with strong, active heart and soul he will be able to meet the future tasks of mankind. Let us, therefore, seek to acquire spiritual science as a language and then wait until, in this language, we find the questions which we may put to the Christ. And He will answer. *Yes, He will* answer!

Abundant will be the forces, sustenance and impulses of soul which — out of the gray spiritual depths of this time of human development — will be received by those who will hear the counsel that He will give in the near future to those who seek for it.[11]

———

Ideas are for spiritual knowledge, for Anthroposophy, the lovingly wrought vessels within which is gathered in a spiritual way, out of spiritual worlds, the *true being of man*. Held and enclosed in lovingly-formed thoughts, the light of true humanity seeks to shine out through Anthroposophy. For knowledge is only the form in which it is made possible, through man, for the truth of the spirit to be gathered out of the wide reaches of the world-all and stored in human hearts, so that out of human hearts it can illuminate human thinking.

And because Anthroposophy can really be grasped only through love, it is therefore love-creating, when it is grasped by men in its true nature.

And words, in the anthroposophical sphere, are not formulated as is common today.... Every word in Anthroposophy, when it is rightly expressed, is in reality an asking, a reverent plea — a plea that the spirit may descend to human beings.[12]

———

In earlier times, the relationship between the *living* and the *so-called dead* was a much closer one, in a natural, although not fully conscious way, than it is today. The influence of materialism has been to weaken and gradually to sever this bond. But in the future a bridge will be built once again, consciously, to those who have died.

For those who have passed through death need and long for the love and the thoughts of those who were close to them on the earth. Although they find themselves surrounded by the light of the spirit, they need also what the living can give them. Yet material thoughts have little reality for them, and so do not reach them.... Loving, light-filled *spiritual thoughts*, on the other hand, are like *nourishment* for them, without which they go hungry. And there is often much hunger of this kind today among those who are experiencing the life after death.

Thus we can help and work not only for those who live on the earth, but also for those who live between death and a new birth, through the life-filled, spirit-filled thoughts which we bring to them.

On the other hand, this relationship is by no means one-sided; for those who have died can in turn be of very real help to the living. For one part of the task, the occupation, of the so-called dead, is that their gaze, their spiritual gaze, now turns toward those who still live upon the earth; that with their forces they observe those upon the earth — that the souls living upon the earth are perceived by the souls who have died. Through spiritual science men will learn the meaning of such words as these: *Those who have passed through the gate of death gaze upon me, they imbue me with life, they are with me, their forces stream down upon me.* And men will learn to speak of the dead as ones who live, who are spiritually living.

Through spiritual science we learn to feel responsibility for all that we do in relationship to the dead; but we learn to know also the deep feeling of blessing that comes when we can say to ourselves: "At this moment you are doing this or that, but, as you do so, one or the other who has died beholds you with his active powers; his forces grow together with your own." Not that the dead *give* us the forces; these we must develop ourselves. The one who has died, who is between death and a new birth, does not give us our talents; we must have these. But he is a very real and active help, as if he stood there behind us.

And indeed he does really stand there behind us.[13]

Intelligence is the reciprocal interrelationship of spiritual beings — of the higher hierarchies. What they do, how they relate to one another, what they mean to one another, this is *cosmic intelligence*. And since we, as human beings, must look to the realm which is nearest above us, so, for us, concretely spoken, cosmic intelligence is the sum of the spiritual beings of the hierarchy of the angels. When we speak concretely, we cannot speak of a sum of intelligence, but of a sum of angels; this is the reality....

All that we call a physical planet is an assemblage of spiritual beings. When we look up to a star, that which appears to us physically is only its outer manifestation; in reality we have to do there with a congregation of spiritual beings.

There we have, on the one hand, sun-intelligences, and on the other, planetary-intelligences. And it has ever been so, that the sun-intelligence stands under the rulership of Michael, while the other planetary-intelligences are ruled by the other archangels.[14]

How do Michael and Ahriman* stand in relation to one another, we may ask, inasmuch as both are active in the development of man's intellectual powers?

Ahriman acquired intellectuality at a far distant time in cosmic evolution when he could not make it an inward experience within himself. It remains, therefore, a force in him which has nothing to do with heart and soul. Thus as a cold, frosty, soulless cosmic impulse, intellectuality now streams out from Ahriman.

Michael, on the other hand, has never acquired intellectuality for himself. He reigns over it as a divine spiritual force, while feeling himself united with the divine spiritual powers. He bears within him all the primordial forces of the higher spiritual beings and of man. Thus he confers upon the intellect nothing cold, frosty, or soulless, but guards it in a way that is warm, intimate and soul-filled.

As an imaginative image this can be described:

Michael — the Spiritual Being who guides our present era — reigns through the course of time, bearing the *light of the cosmos* as the *life* of his own being — giving form to the warmth of the cosmos as the revelation of his own being. He wends like a world, yea-saying himself only inasmuch as he says *yea* to the world, as if guiding down from every dwelling place of the cosmos forces to the earth.

---

*Ahriman: from the Persian, meaning Dark Spirit. Another designation of Michael and Ahriman is the centuries-old image of Saint Michael and the Dragon.

The opposing Spirit, Ahriman, would in his course *wrest space away from time.* He harbors darkness about him into which he projects the rays of his own light; the more he achieves his ends, the keener grows the frost about him; he moves like a world that contracts into *one* single being — his own, yea-saying himself only by *nay*-saying the world, moving as though he drew with him sinister forces from the dark caverns of the earth....

Man, however — when as a free being he draws near to Michael — begins to carry the forces of his intellectuality right down into his *entire human being.* He thinks indeed with his head, but his heart feels the light and dark of his thought, and his will now rays out the whole of his being, because his thought streams fully through him, not as shadowy intellect but as purpose and goal. Man grows ever more man as he grows to be an expression of the world; he finds himself, *not* by *seeking himself*, which isolates him, but when, through the activity of his will, he unites himself in love with the world.... For man only experiences himself truly when he loves the world.

These imaginations arise out of man's love for what he does (Michael), or his love of himself in doing (Ahriman)....

And when love for Michael, who remains ever true to cosmic intelligence, is present, then love of the world is cultivated. It becomes possible *to love without self-love*; and upon this path Christ can be found by the human soul.

Thus Michael is the guide to the Christ Being.

The dawn of the Michael age has broken. *Hearts are beginning to have thoughts.* Enthusiasm no longer springs from mere mystical darkness, but from thought-upborne clearness of soul. To understand this means to take Michael into the heart. — Thought that would strive to grasp the spirit must spring from hearts that beat for Michael, as the fire-spending thought-prince of the universe.[15]

REFERENCES

and

INDEX

QUOTATION REFERENCES

0. *This information concerning the cover design was kindly provided by Peter Stebbing.*
1. *Wahrspruchworte,* Page 114.
2. *Ways to a New Style in Architecture,*
   Lecture 2, Dornach, June 17, 1914.
3. *The Elemental Beings which are Connected with Beauty, Goodness and Truth,*
   Dornach, December 16, 1922.
4. *The Nature of Color,*
   Part II, Dornach, July 29, 1923.
5. *Spiritual Knowledge,*
   Oxford, August 20, 1922.
6. *Ways to a New Style in Architecture,*
   Lecture 2, Dornach, June 17, 1914.
7. *The Plastic Arts,*
   Lecture 3, Haag, April 19, 1922.
8. *The World of the Senses and the World of the Spirit,*
   Lecture 1, Hannover, December 27, 1911.
9. *The Nature of Color,*
   Part II, Dornach, December 5, 1920; July 29, 1923.
10. *Love and its Meaning in the World,*
    Zurich, December 17, 1912.
11. *Cosmic and Human Metamorphoses,*
    Berlin, February 6, 1917.
12. *Words of Pain and the Searching of Conscience,*
    Stuttgart, January 25, 1923. (Not in English)
13. *Links Between the Living and the Dead,*
    Two lectures, Bergen, October 10, 11, 1913.
14. *Karma Lectures,*
    Volume III, August 8, 1924.
15. *The Michael Mystery,*
    Letters 9 and 1.

The italicizing in the prose passages is the translator's.

English Titles and First Lines

A Secret of Nature	41
All forces are but empty husks	55
At the Ringing of the Bells	13
At the turn of time	107
Behold the plant	41
Behold the sun	29
Being sprung from the world-all	37
Bind yourself to matter	15
Child's Evening Prayer	81
Christmas	27, 29
Darkness, Light, Love	15
Easter	35
Ecce Homo	9
For the Dead	89
From my head to my feet	81
From out the Godhead sprang the human soul	69
Glory to God in the heights	27
Good and Evil, a fairytale	147
Grace	41
He must give up his separate life and being	67
I gaze into the darkness	65
I look into the world	85
I was united with you	97
I would enkindle every man	77
If man fully knows himself	71
In light we are guiding	19
In radiant light	95
In the ether ocean's color shimmer	43
In the heart the weaving feeling	9
In the light-filled air of spirit lands	45
In the light of world-all thoughts	91

In Time of Illness	53
Into spirit pastures I will send	93
Light and Star	11
Love and Hate, a fairytale	124
Man finds	67
Man looks out	47
May my love be interwoven	91
Michael-Imagination	25
Michael's Sword	23
More radiant than the sun	65
Morning Verse, Grades 1-4	83
Morning Verse, Grades 5-12	85
O Man	23
O Thou, God's Spirit, fill me full	53
Out of the Spirit, all being has sprung	75
Out of the Spirit's luminous heights	73
Phantasy, a fairytale	154
Seek in your own being	61
Soul of man!	101-111
Spirits of your souls *(May be used also in the singular.)*	89
Spiritual Communion	33
Spring	21
Stand before man's great life-portal	35
Stars spoke of old to men	31
Sun-all-mighty offspring	25
Sun, you radiance-harborer	63
The Cloud-Illuminator	51
The Deity has given me my "I"	53
The forces of man are dual in nature	55
The Foundation Stone	99
The Goetheanum wanted	71
The human soul has need of inward trust	51
The light of the sun is flooding	115

The love of my soul	93
The One who has Died Speaks	95
The Rock-Spring-Wonder, a fairytale	141
The seeds are quickened in the night of the earth	41
The soul of the world lies out-stretched	75
The soul's clear eye reflects	27
The soul's questings are quickening	57
The sun's bright beam	21
The sun with loving light	83
The weaving essence of the light streams forth	130
There come to me in earth's activity	33
They light up like stars	11
Through tangling soul-hindrances	39
Tintagel	69
To bind oneself to matter	15
To the Berlin Friends	47
To turn us towards the light	11
To us it is given	17
To wonder at beauty	13
We come from old impressive ruined castles	69
When in warmth of love	59
Where sense perception ends	39
Whitsun	39
World-Soul-Spirits	19
You, who watch over the souls of the spheres	89

German Titles and First Lines

Abendgebet für Kinder	80
Aus dem Geiste ist alles Sein entsprungen	74
Aus des Geistes lichten Höhen	72
Aus Gottessein erstand die Menschenseele	68
Beim Läuten der Glocken	12
Das Schöne bewundern	12
Dem Stoff sich verschreiben	14
Den Berliner Freunden	46
Der Mensch findet	66
Der Sonne liebes Licht	82
Der Sonnenstrahl	20
Der Tote Spricht	94
Der Wolkendurchleuchter	50
Des Menschen Kräfte sind zweifach geartet	54
Die Ihr wachet über Sphärenseelen	88
Die Kräfte sind leere Hülsen nur	54
Die Sonne schaue	28
Durch schwere Seelenhindernisse	38
Ecce Homo	8
Ein Geheimnis der Natur	40
Ein Ich gab mir das Göttliche	52
Erkennt der Mensch sich selbst	70
Es bedarf der Mensch der innern Treue	50
Es keimen der Seele Wünsche	56
Es keimen die Pflanzen	40
Es leuchtet gleich Sternen	10
Es muss sein Sondersein und Leben opfern	66
Es nahet mir im Erdenwirken	32
Es offenbart die Weltenseele sich	74
Es siehet der Mensch	46
Es strebe zu dir meiner Seele Liebe	92

Es wollte im Sinnenstoffe	70
Finsternis, Licht, Liebe	14
Frühling	20
Für die Toten	88
Gebet für Kranke	52
Geister eurer Seelen	88
Geistige Kommunion	32
Grundsteinspruch	100
Ich möchte jeden Menschen	76
Ich schaue in die Finsternis	64
Ich schaue in die Welt	84
Ich war mit euch vereint	96
Im Farbenschein des Äthermeeres	42
Im Leuchtenden	94
Im Lichte der Weltgedanken	90
Im Lichte wir schalten	18
Im Seelenaug' sich spiegelt	26
In dem Herzen webet Fühlen	8
In der Lichtesluft des Geisterlandes	44
In der Zeitenwende	106
In Geistgefilde will ich senden	92
Licht und Stern	10
Meine Liebe sei den Hüllen	90
Menschenseele!	100–110
Michael-Imagination	24
Michaels Schwert	22
Morgenspruch	82, 84
O Gottesgeist erfülle mich	52
O Mensch	22
Offenbarung durch die Höhe dem Gotte	26
Ostern	34
Pfingsten	38
Schaue die Pflanze!	40

Sonne, du strahlentragende	62
Sonnenmächten Entsprossene	24
Steh' vor des Menschen Lebenspforte	34
Sterne sprachen einst zu Menschen	30
Strahlender als die Sonne	64
Suche im eigenen Wesen	60
Tintagel	68
Tischgebet	40
Uns ist gegeben	16
Von Kopf bis zum Fuss	80
Von vielsagenden Burgestrümmern kommen wir	68
Weihnacht	26
Weltenseelengeister	18
Weltentsprossenes Wesen, du in Lichtgestalt	36
Wenn der Mensch, warm in Liebe	58
Wintersonnenwende	28
Wo Sinneswissen endet	38
Zum Lichte uns zu wenden	10

www.ingramcontent.com/pod-product-compliance
Lightning Source LLC
Chambersburg PA
CBHW022059160426
43198CB00008B/290